HAPPY CLOUD MEDIA LLC  PRESENTS:

# EXPLOITATION N

...ploitation Nation is published by Happy Cloud Media, LLC
Vol. 1, No. 1 © 2017

Amy Lynn Best, Publisher
Mike Watt, Editor
Carolyn Haushalter, Asst. Editor

Contributors:
Bill Adcock
Dr. Rhonda Baughman
Mike Haushalter
Bill Homan
Douglas Waltz
William Wright

Cover art designed by
Ryan Hose

Cover photo by
David Cooper
Models: Amy Lynn Best
Sofiya Smirnova

Special Thanks to:
Clive Barker
Bill Hahner
Mark Miller
Scooter McCrae
Pete Chiarella

**Exploitation Nation is published quarterly by Happy Cloud Media, LLC, (Amy Lynn Best & Mike Watt, PO Box 1540, McMurray, PA 15317).** Exploitation Nation Issue #1 (ISBN 1548718904 ) is copyright 2017 by Happy Cloud Media LLC. All rights reserved. All featured articles and illustrations are copyright 2017 by their respective writers and artists. Reproductions of any material in whole or in part without its creator's written permission is strictly forbidden. Exploitation Nation accepts no responsibility for unsolicited manuscripts, DVDs, stills, art, or any other materials. Contributions are accepted on an invitational basis only.

**Visit Us At Facebook.Com/ExploitationNation**

# DOWN THE RABBIT HOLE

Not to be an alarmist, but these are some desperate times we're living in. Between the political and economic upheaval the world faces, all we have to distract ourselves from the angry Facebook arguments is simple entertainment, and fortunately there's no shortage of that. Unfortunately, for fans of gore and sleaze, the entertainment business is quickly becoming a vast wasteland.

And that's puzzling because as of this writing there are more means of entertainment delivery than ever before: Hulu, Vudu, YouTube, Vimeo, Roku— that's just naming the services that end in vowels, not even taking Amazon or Netflix into consideration—there should be no end of boredom relief. But while more movies and long-form episodic series are pouring out of our TV screens, so much of it is recent, and movies both classic and "classic" are once again disappearing into the mists of time. What to do if you're in the mood for a Jess Franco or a Lucio Fulci and you don't have the DVD in your collection? Maybe you could find it on an outlying Roku station, but most likely you're, as they say in the business, shit out of luck. But *Captain America: Civil War*? Try to avoid it, I defy you.

Even as the era of physical media seems to be on the decline, there are multiple DVD heroes out there keeping the best and worst in print. Severin Films and Vinegar Syndrome have dedicated themselves to not only preserving the sleaze of days-gone-by but remastering them well beyond even the filmmakers' wildest dreams. Did you ever think you'd see the day when *The Sinful Dwarf, Dr. Butcher M.D.,* or *Manos Hands of Fate* would wind up on Blu-Ray? Synapse just released the video staple *Popcorn* (in a large part due to horror hero Kristy Jett) in a schmancy tin box, remastered and rife with extras, but pricey, and that just adds to the problem. Too few hardcore horror fans have the disposable income necessary to keep their collections in the size we've grown accustomed. The demand just isn't there to keep the prices lower, and lesser-known and/or loved movies are falling by the wayside. It's no wonder that VHS is making a comeback. We're not likely to see *Small Kill* on DVD any time soon. (Of course, I thought the same thing about the Micky Dolenz-starring thriller *Night of the Strangler*, but thanks to Vinegar Syndrome, it's within our grasp.)

Which brings us to the crux of the problem: the fanbase for exploitation of old is shrinking. I witness this firsthand with my students at Pittsburgh Filmmakers. Too few of the so-called Millennial Generation seem to care about anything made prior to 1990. Touting the oeuvre of H.G. Lewis or Ted V. Mikels results in a rousing response of indifference. Hitchcock and Welles will always be kings, but the exploit-eers are in grave danger of being forgotten entirely. But maligning the interests of the previous generation is nothing new. How many of us, the Gen-Xers and Gen-Ys, flock to the filmographies of William Wyler or Howard Hawks? Every generation is guilty of neglecting the art of days gone by.

The lurid world of exploitation— those films who hang their plots on the elements of sex, violence, gore, nudity, and property damage—is going untended, weeds growing up and choking out the flowering blossoms of antisocial filmmaking. Though horror conventions are devolving into autograph shows propped up on the popularity of *The Walking Dead*, you can still hear hearty cries of "Troma!" echoing through the dealer's rooms. Those exhortations are clarion calls to the like-minded. Our numbers may be shrinking, but we're still here. We still matter.

So that's where *Exploitation Nation* comes in. Within these pages, we'll be touting the merits of the best and worst of, for lack of a better umbrella, "genre" films. *La La Land* be damned, Roger Corman produced better stories about "white people discovering jazz" with the added benefit of complete lack of Ryan Gosling. But *Bucket of Blood* was never nominated for an Academy Award. Still, there's always hope.

2017 has already seen the arrival of throwbacks like *The Love Witch* and *The Greasy Strangler*, and we're only halfway through the year. If we're not nuked by North Korea by this time next year, who knows what wonders we'll have witnessed?

*Exploitation Nation* stands with publications like *Shock Cinema, Videoscope, Evilspeak, Ultra-Violent,* and *Grindhouse Purgatory*, dedicated to the weird, bizarre, and unsavory.

This premiere issue focuses primarily on the wonderful world of lesbian vampire films (with many other tidbits scattered throughout). Upcoming issues will tackle the insanity of the mid-80s, early-'90s Hong Kong action boom, the Scream Queen era, the "Video Nasty" hysteria, and other magical times of peak sleaze. We'll also do our best to indicate where and how (and *if*) you can obtain these marvelous records of unsavory history.

   –   Mike Watt, May, 2017

# A CONVERSATION WITH DYANNE THORNE
## By William Wright

Arguably, there is no character in the history of exploitation cinema as iconic and infamous as the central, titular villain of drive-in auteur Don Edmonds' hyper-violent and hyper-sexual *Ilsa* series. Loosely based on the real-life Nazi war criminal, Ilse Koch, wife of concentration camp commandant, Karl Koch, whose boundless cruelty and macabre "hobby" of collecting "souvenirs" from the bodies of prisoners earned her the fearsome moniker of "*Die Hexe von Buchenwald*" ("The Witch of Buchenwald"), Edmonds' cold-hearted creation served as both the paradigm and pinnacle of the "women in prison" and "Nazisploitaion" sub-genres of the 1970s. 1975's *Ilsa, She-Wolf of the SS*, regarded by exploitation aficionados as the purest distillation of the character, portrays Ilsa as the coldly beautiful and iron-handed commandant of a Nazi prisoner of war camp with a bizarrely feminist agenda. In an effort to prove that women have a superior endurance to pain and should therefore be allowed active combat roles in the war, she conducts inhuman scientific experiments on her inmates. Ilsa's cruelty in the name of the Reich is rivaled only by her voracious sexual appetite and quest to find a man who can match her unquenchable libido—

all who fail find themselves liberated of their testicles. Despite Ilsa's apparent death in *Ilsa, She Wolf of the SS*, grindhouse and drive-in audiences would be treated to further sinister adventures of the sadistic femme fatale in two official sequels: *Ilsa, Harem Keeper of the Oil Sheiks* (1976), which found a new incarnation of the character trafficking in sexual slavery for a Middle-Eastern monarch, and *Ilsa, the Tigress of Siberia* (1977), in which Ilsa is the supervisor of a gulag during the last days of Stalin.

With widely varying timelines and settings, the *Ilsa* films are consistent in the one element that elevates them from mere exploitation to true drive-in gems: actress Dyanne Thorne. She was already a veteran of the "B" movie scene of the late '60s and early '70s having appeared in such exploitation and soft-core films as *The Erotic Adventures of Pinocchio* (1971), *Point of Terror* (1971), and *Blood Sabbath* (1972) as well as numerous TV appearances ranging from *Car 54, Where Are You?* to *Star Trek* before taking on her signature role Hitler's estrogen-fueled fury. Nevertheless, Ilsa will forever be the role that defines Dyanne Thorne. Thorne owns Ilsa in a way that few actors own career-defining roles,

4

elevating the character through her performance above and beyond the mere sex and violence of of the admittedly audacious and controversial subject matter, and, in turn, injecting the sadistic, sex-starved Nazi she-devil with, if not actual pathos, a definite sense of pity. It is impossible to imagine another actress in Ilsa's jackboots—so much so that she was cast in Jess (*Vampyros Lesbos*) Franco's 1977 *Ilsa* knock-off, *Greta, the Torturer*, released in the U.S. as *Ilsa, the Wicked Warden*. With the resurgence of interest in gritty, '70s style exploitation fare thanks to films such as Rob Zombie's *The Devil's Rejects* and Quentin Tarantino and Robert Rodriguez's brilliantly grand failure, *Grindhouse* (in which Thorne was cast for *Werewolf Women of the SS*, but ultimately turned down due to, by her own account, less than stellar treatment from Weinstein Company representatives), *Ilsa* is once again on the pop culture map. I recently caught up with Dyanne Thorne, who, now in her 70s, remains stunning. Beautiful, vivacious and still in possession of Ilsa's legendarily dangerous curves, she exudes the energy and confidence of a woman half her age. And thankfully, she's nothing like her onscreen alter ego. Having spent the last decade pursuing interests outside of film including stage work, attaining a doctorate in comparative religion, and running a successful "alternative" wedding business in Las Vegas with her musician/actor husband Howard Maurer, Thorne is well aware of the dangers of revisiting her most notorious role. "The *Ilsa* roles were great fun while they were there, but if you have a profitable business elsewhere, to put that business in jeopardy because some people from the other side of the line don't quite understand those films and may look at a squarer vision of you, it could really hamper your business," Thorne says. "So, I was living a really conservative life -- and I'm not in any way pointing a finger at myself as an actress except for the stage work which is all comedy and harmless." Above all, Dyanne Thorne is the consummate professional taking on every endeavor with enthusiasm and dedication. With a formal education in acting—something that many of her grindhouse and "B" movie contemporaries lacked—Thorne's dedication to her craft goes back to her formative years. Thorne speaks fondly of those early days and of the challenges that led to her professional career. "I was going to NYU and they had a wonderful theatre school when I went there, and I met other actors. Everybody was struggling to come up. They were studying with Stella Adler and Lee Strasberg, and I made a choice to do the same."

However, studying under the internationally acclaimed teachers of "method acting" did take some degree of adjustment on the young actress's part. "At NYU, we were learning the classic, English style (of acting), and they were all getting into method acting, and so, I thought, 'Uh-oh, I need to know something here!' I went to study with Lee Strasberg—a brilliant teacher. He said to me, 'You need a basic technique' because now I had to unlearn the English technique. I was working in a different way. He told me, 'It's hampering you.'"

*All Photos this section Dyanne Thorne in **Ilsa: She-Wolf of the SS.***
*Copyright Cambist Films. All Rights Reserved*

At that point, Strasberg made a surprising recommendation. "Although, they didn't like each other, he said, 'Stella Adler would be good for you.' So, I studied with her and she opened a door for me with a wonderful director. She introduced us and he had a film—I was not yet a member of any union—and she said,'I think you would be very good for it.' And I looked older than my age. Although I was just 20, this role was for a 30 year-old. There was no problem for me to play it."

That big break would foreshadow Thorne's future roles in one very specific way. "I was to have been the second wife to a very wealthy man that I got to murder at the end! It was called *Encounter* and it was a decent film," says Thorne. *Encounter* would also feature another actor who would go on to much great success. "(In the film) this man supposedly had a child, before I killed him off, of course, who was little Bobby DeNiro! And that's how he was billed, 'Little Bobby DeNiro'."

However, with *Encounter*, Dyanne Thorne learned a harsh, early lesson about the financial side of indie filmmaking. "They ran out of money when it came time for distribution," says Thorne. "They took it to South America and it became a monster! It did very, very well, but I never did see my money. What I had was a contract that said when they sell it, I would get this many dollars and I'll continue to get this percentage. Well, that's like a joke! You'd think I would have learned my lesson because I did ten more things like that in my lifetime and I never did see a penny from any of them!"

Despite her long list of movie credits, Dyanne Thorne considers herself something of an "accidental" film actress but always willing to go where the work took her. "I'm a stage actress," she says. "When I started to do film, it wasn't really something I pursued. I pursued television because it was easy money. They were never really important roles—they were a lot of comedy things, so it was light and bright and easily done. I pursued the stage work, so, when the opportunities that have come to me in film, it was never something that I was out there seeking."

Thorne has found that those opportunities can come from often unlikely sources. "I did a thing called

6

*Point of Terror* with Alex (*The Screaming Skull*) Nichol—a wonderful film with Peter Carpenter. We had a lot of fun doing it. My hairdresser was Peter Carpenter's hairdresser and recom-mended me to his producer who took it to Crown International, and they said that I looked like a good fit. But, these weren't things I was looking for, although the independents were getting popular then and getting into independents without looking for work was easy—they were looking for actresses. So, my reputation led me to getting other work, "Thorne explains. "It wasn't major studio stuff, but it was independent and everyone treated you just first class. I have absolutely no regrets. Every single film I did which led up to doing the *Ilsa* films was a joy. That's a 'square' word, but it really has been fun and it doesn't do anybody any harm. What's the point in doing it if you're not having any fun?" A self-described "workaholic," Dyanne Thorne has a relentless work ethic and her addiction to a job well-done is a habit she has no intention of breaking. "I have to work. That's my nature. When you talk about a film like Don Edmonds' *Ilsa, She-Wolf of the SS*, we did it in nine days! After nine days, I can't sit back for the rest of the year waiting for work, so, I jumped into a play." As far as preferring the medium of film over the stage, Thorne is surprisingly pragmatic. "It's all just an acting job," Thorne says. "But it is fun to get the applause [and] that immediate response, then you know if they hate you or they love you. With *Ilsa*, you never really know!"

No one is more surprised at *Ilsa*'s enduring popularity than Thorne herself. "Who knew that it was going to be what it is? The first time I saw that someone wrote 'She's the mistress of mayhem! She's the female James Bond,' I went, 'What?!' I didn't realize the role called for that! You just do the role and it's always fun to see where it leads. But *nobody* expected it to be what it is now. I'm grateful."

She does, however, attribute much of her success to her wildly devoted fanbase. "I have the sweetest fans in the world. When I look at other actresses who have had mainstream success, they don't have the fun I have! They're scared to death to connect with their fans—the ones who do TV shows won't even accept a gift. People don't know that. They don't even open them! They are terrified of what might be. The people that I have commingled with (at conventions), and the letters that I receive... It's really beyond my understanding how I ever merited getting as much mail as I get. They have been sweet people. Some may ask, 'Don't you get negative mail?' No. I can't find a negative letter that has come in. It's heartwarming. So, that's made doing those films that much more fun."

Given the current political and social climate in the United States, an obvious question is could a film like *Ilsa* be made today? Dyanne Thorne prefers to take a neutral stance. "I'm not into politics at all," she states. The *Ilsa* actress suggests that other entertainers would do well to follow her example. "In fact, I remember Stella Adler saying, 'It's an actor's job to mind your own business.' Because you are a role-model. If you're wrong, if you lead the public to a candidate because you feel strongly, you need to be moralistic about everything you do—totally ethical... Political climate is a very sensitive thing these days. It's like spirituality; who can tell you what to believe?"

Nevertheless, Thorne refuses to remain silent on some hot-button issues. "I received a letter from some folks in England who were just appalled to know that stories about the Holocaust are being taken out of the textbooks because it's *offending* people from the Middle East. I don't understand that. You can't change history." Ironically, *Ilsa* has become a tool for fighting anti-semitism in those countries bent on revising history. " ...There's a group pushing the *Ilsa* films in the underground so that they can be reminded of what took place," Thorne reveals. "You can't change history and you can't bury it, and there are people who don't want their kids to know it or people who doubt it who need to be reminded that this is a reality."

And according to Thorne, "reality" has always been of prime importance in all of the *Ilsa* films. "*Greta* was a reality of what took place in a sanitarium where women who were sent there were tortured by a real wicked warden. That was a true thing. The same with *Oil Sheiks*. Don

Edmonds did research on it and that was when college students were being kidnapped to be harem girls in the Middle East. We don't think about that, but it took place, like it or not, it *did* take place. There's a lot of stuff going on even now. I'm ashamed at our country when you look at the statistics of people who are being forced into slavery—*in our own country*—it's just a different kind of slavery. Does the political climate warrant another *Ilsa*? Maybe it does!"

As a student of humanity and history, Dyanne Thorne did not create her performance as Ilsa in a vacuum. She did her research, but found the facts too horrid to aid in her characterization in any meaningful way and might have eventually proven to be an impediment. "The first thing I did was go to the second hand bookstore and come home with all these books on Ilse Koch," says Thorne. "It really didn't give me much except to know that I had better stop reading because you can't play a role if you judge the character, and I started judging this woman and that's not helpful. I did get a touch of the history and what she went through and where she'd come from and that she was serious about it. I found it hard to believe that anyone could be that cruel, maybe because it was a woman, you think, 'okay, *men* do that, but *women don't do that!*' That just gave me more ammunition so I could take that passion, if you will, that she had for destruction and put it into the character and that hopefully let me play a role of a woman who was powerful despite the fact that she used it in a negative way. I hope that power came through, and perhaps, it did."

However, inhabiting Ilsa's skin was not without its uncomfortable moments. As graphic as the final cut of *Ilsa, She-Wolf of the SS* is, only a fraction of the depravity of the script made it to the screen. "There were many pages that I refused to do, and there were others that we made adjustments to that they had other people do. Yes, you do feel uncomfortable about some things, and other times, being uncomfortable is exactly what you need to get what you want out of the script." Thorne also took issue with the screenplay's structure. "*Ilsa* was written like a monologue almost," says Thorne. "I often said 'Give this line to someone else. Let's have some conversation here!' The script really was the worst!"

On the subject of the resurgence of gritty, '70s style drive-in fare, Dyanne Thorne chooses her words carefully. The "how and why" of the sudden popularity is of little concern to the actress. Nevertheless, she is grateful for the renewed interest. "Oh, don't ask me that! I cannot imagine. . . Maybe it's an escape from the reality of the news filling our heads every day that this is the last day of our lives. Maybe it's a wonderful escape; we see something worse that makes us feel a little better. You'd have to ask a psychologist about that. I really don't know! But, I'm glad that it is (popular again) because I wouldn't be here talking to you if it weren't!"

With a lifetime of experience in independent cinema, Dyanne Thorne's advice to the current crop of "B" movie actresses is simple. "Just be smart. We give ourselves away these days for free. I think we've lost respect for ourselves in many ways. Any mistake that I've made is because I didn't take the time to investigate who I was working with. Half of the mistakes that I made could have been avoided if I had been smarter. I think

that I if you're well-trained at whatever it is you do, and if you have

a passion and you like to do it, you'll succeed. Emerson had a quote: 'Where the interest lies, there lies the talent. Where you develop the talent, there lies the success.' I was teaching acting for a while, and I said, 'I can't do this anymore' because I would do all this preparation, and we would get ready to do a show, and we would bring the kids in... They wouldn't even read the full play or the full movie script! They just read their part and their idea was 'I want to be a star. I don't want to be an actor. I don't want to study. I don't want to improve my diction. I am who I am.' Well, that's wonderful, but that's very limiting. Once you don't have that particular role anymore, you just don't go out there and be a star. Stars have said before that it takes years to become a star 'overnight' and I truly believe that. Look at this! At a time when I was *totally* rejected for *Ilsa*, here I am with thousands of people saying 'thanks for being Ilsa.' It took years for that to turn itself around, and for that I am grateful."

It's going on 25 years since I began my career as an "entertainment journalist", the clumsy name I gave for writing about movies and those who made them, writing for major print publications like *Cinefantastique, Femme Fatales, Fangoria, The Dark Side,* and, my first love, *Film Threat.*

During that time, I'd been assigned stories that were eventually bumped for space considerations. Or editorial decisions. Or "just because." The following pieces were commissioned by *Cinefantastique* for what was, at the time, an exciting development: a number of Clive Barker's comic book stories were being developed as TV movies for the SyFy Channel (or, then, "The Sci-Fi Channel") and the first of these was to be a new story based on a comic book title that Barker liked, but hadn't been particularly happy with. The title, *Saint Sinner,* was reworked to tell the story of a medieval monk who follows a pair of demons into our modern day to stop the end of the world.

Hooked up with Barker and three major stars (I cannot for the life of me locate Greg Serrano's interview), I turned in a combined 10,000 words to my *CFQ* editor. But word-on-the-street had it that the producers of the movie weren't entirely thrilled with the finished film. I don't know if that affected the decision to kill the coverage or if it was a space thing.

For whatever reason, the three interviews were reworked into a single piece. *Saint Sinner* premiered on Sci-Fi in October, 2002, to underwhelming critical reviews and tepid viewership. Which is unfortunate, since the movie is clever and introduces some interesting concepts *vis a vis* the relationship between the Judeo-Christian God and his opposite number in "Hell", and what those concepts could actually mean.

*Saint Sinner* is available on DVD for those who wish to fill holes in their Clive Barker history. It will become apparent to those reading that many of the projects here—the proposed *Lord of Illusions* and *Ecto-Kid* TV series', the *Twisted Souls* movie—never came to fruition, while Barker's *Abarat* series now numbers three, with the 2011 publication of *Absolute Midnight.* On the other hand, Shout Factory put out a lovely "almost-director's cut" of *Nightbreed* in 2015.

While the theme of this first issue is "lesbian vampire", the two female demons have a very, shall we say, "close relationship" (which may actually be incestuous as well), so we'll bend the concept a bit and hammer these in to fit. So for the first time ever, here are the uncut interviews I conducted with Clive Barker, Mary Mara, and Rebecca Harrell.

## CLIVE BARKER TALKS "SAINT SINNER"

[2002] is going to be an exciting year for Clive Barker fans. There are new projects around every corner, new nightmares to bite and haunt and thrill. On the heels of his latest novel, *Coldheart Canyon*, which was nominated for an award by International Horror Guild, his next book is called *Abarat*, what he calls "the first of my quartet for children and fantasists of all ages" and will feature over a hundred brand-new oil paintings by the author and artist himself. And there are movies. Adding to the canon of *Hellraiser, Candyman* will be new cinematic delights and despairs. The first of which will air in October on the Sci-Fi Channel: *Saint Sinner*.

Sound familiar? Well, not exactly *Saint Sinner*, written for the screen by

*Dark Angel* scribe Doris Egan and directed by Joshua Butler, *Saint Sinner* is a brand-new tale for the screen, and not an adaptation of the long-lamented and laid-to-rest Marvel Comic book of the same title.

"Not even vaguely related," Barker says, "Except that the title was cool. I was always disappointed with the way that Marvel handled that entire line of comics, particularly *Saint Sinner*. And I thought 'that's a waste of a good title'. It was something that called for finding a new life in some way or another. I had a deal over at Fox Television for a while, and though nothing came of that deal in terms of actual programming, we had gotten to the point where they had said to [Barker's film company] Seraphim, 'what we want is we'd like to be in the business of making movies of the week again'. It turns out they made none of them for anyone. But what it did was cause me to create six stories for that venue. One of them was *Saint Sinner*, and it existed in this twenty-five page treatment. When we came to talk to the Sci-Fi Channel, it turned out that they really did want to make movies. I said 'I've got this one that I think is really cool'. It found a life over there."

It will come as a surprise to no one that *Saint Sinner* is a tale of darkness. A young eighteenth-century monk accidentally unleashes a pair of female demons, and has to follow them into our modern world and stop them from laying waste to humanity. The word is *Saint Sinner* will push the television limits of violence and sexuality to their extent and beyond. In other words, no one pulled any punches with this one. "Oh man, yeah! You know what kind of enthusiast [director Joshua (*Prancer Returns*) Butler] is. He's an expert in the genre. He said to me very clearly 'I want to make sure this is true to the Clive Barker tradition', if you will. It was very important to him right from the outset that this be a picture that did not disappoint the Clive Barker fans. There will be a host of new Josh Butler fans when it comes out. I think he's done something really special."

At the center of the film are the two demons, Nakir and Munkar (played by Rebecca Harrell and Mary Mara, respectively). They are ancient beings who have chosen the form of women to feed on humanity. Together, they represent multiple dualities—mother and daughter, teacher and pupil—and have every potential to be new Barker-inspired fan favorites.

"It's a demon-driven show, no question," Barker says with a laugh. "The two dark angels, Nakir and Munkar. The names are not inventions. They're actually real angels on the dark side, according to my *Bruster's Book of Mythology*. There is very little else in the way of detail about them. The medieval scholars and theologians loved invent angels and demons and enumerate them. This was like one of the medieval pastimes. I found these two names and they were always twinned: the idea that the two of them were always together was very interesting to me. And then making them both women was just, I thought, fun. So very, very seldom still do villains get to be villainesses. And I've had very good experiences, both in my books and on the screen—I'm thinking of Julia in the first two *Hellraiser* movies—with infernal women. "Infernal" in the sense of "from the inferno". And so it seemed like a cool fun thing to do. And there's an extra energy that comes from having women playing these two roles. There's a kind of sexual energy that comes into it, a perverse energy that comes from seeing these two very attractive women made monstrous and doing monstrous deeds. All that's good fun stuff. Playing against type, really. I like to do that. If you can make people sit up and take notice by just not doing the ordinary, it's just fun."

"Ordinary". It's not a word often associated with Clive Barker. That said, *Saint Sinner* has the potential to live or die on the performances of the demons. Surviving that potential pitfall, the movie could easily tank if the director is not up to recreating the visions Barker has set down. These are not fears that Barker has, however.

"Part of the fun for me is [playing against the ordinary] allows the writer and the performers to have a fresh take on what they're doing. I'm reasonably sure that neither Mary nor Rebecca have ever asked to play parts like this in their lives before. And they bring to it the energy of actors who are having fun with something fresh. I think you'll see both of them—there's a yin and yang of what they do. Two sides of a demonic coin, if you will. They're very fun together. I've watched everything that Josh has shot. I'm very, very satisfied. Very pleased, very excited. On every level. In terms of performances, in terms of the look of things, and in terms of what [special effects co-ordinator Patrick Tatopoulos (*Independence Day*)] has provided for us in the way of effects. We are at a new level for this kind of material on television. I think there is something very wonderful going on."

Ultimately, *Saint Sinner* will fit with the other dreams that Barker has created and should prove to be very satisfying. "It has things in common with other material I've done. The presence of demons, the metaphysical layer of the thing. You have a monk teaming with this cop, Dressler, [played by Greg Serano and Gina Ravera] who are completely unalike, going up against these demons, and discovering new things about themselves and each other in the process. For me, the fun thing is there's always this—I don't want to say religious, but metaphysical angle to what I do. What interests me about this kind of material is how many layers it can have. You can be talking about good and evil, you can be talking about pretty heavy subjects and still entertain people. It's something Steve King's done brilliantly over the years—produced an entertainment that has layers to it,

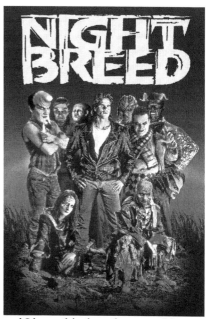

and I hope this does the same thing.

"*Hellraiser* is a movie you can look at two or three ways. *Candyman* is certainly a movie you can look at a number of ways. I'd like to feel that even *Nightbreed*, which I feel is the runt of the litter in the sense of not having ever taken the form that I wanted it to because of producer interference. Nevertheless that is something that is something you can take a number of ways. The gay community very much takes that movie unto itself and says 'this is a metaphor for being gay in our culture'. As a gay man I'm perfectly happy for that interpretation to hold. It's very interesting that these kinds of fictions whether it be horror or fantasy or anything where the imagination is in play is open to lots of interpretation and I find that very fun to play around with."

Barker's happiness with *Saint Sinner* is in direct contrast to his widely-reported dis-satisfaction with the cult film, *Nightbreed*, hence the "runt of the litter" remark. Here is a prime example of Hollywood having no idea what Clive Barker is doing—or wants to do—with his dark stories. In this instance, the seeking of forbidden knowledge has proven detrimental to the seeker. The seeker being Barker, of course, as *Nightbreed*'s writer and director.

"What I know about the making of *Nightbreed* and the dramas and the betrayals and all the nonsenses that go along with making movies, with people who are not always as honest and straightforward as you'd like. To some extent, this all cast a shadow over the movie for me. That shadow doesn't exist for [the audience]. They're actually looking at the picture in a much more straightforward and honest way that I am able to. I do have—there is a history with that movie that makes it difficult for me to even go back and look at the movie. I do know that a lot of people come to signings and say 'that's my favorite movie of yours'. That's very nice. Why do I say it's the runt of the litter? Because there are so many frustrated possibilities there. When you have a vision of something and you get halfway down the line to making it possible and studio politics interfere, it's frustrating. One of these days, I'll buck up the courage and look at it again." People who work on the creative end of filmmaking like to think of the craft as an art-form. Those doling out the money insist it's a business. It's the constant clash of art versus commerce. The sad part is, as any quick glance at a multiplex's marquee will tell you, commerce almost always wins out. "If any other art form as created the same way movies were created, people would shake their heads and say 'that doesn't deserve the term 'art form'. If I was painting a painting and there were twelve people filling in little cards behind me telling me which colors I should using, we would question the validity of the resulting painting. But nobody thinks twice about the fact that a movie has to be tested until every preview card says that it's the best thing since *Citizen Kane*, and 'by the way I don't like this bit so take it out'. I don't think of myself as being that stymied in my relationship with Hollywood. It's just that when you do fail to get the vision on screen, it hurts. Particularly when as a painter and as a writer, I get to do exactly as I want and nobody fucks around with me. That's a big difference! When I turn in a book, sure my editor is there with notes and naturally a lot of time I will put those notes through, but nobody's ever saying to me 'you have to do this'. The same with the paintings. I have great creative freedoms there. So it feels more frustrating when you get to a medium that has so many possibilities and yet has so many cooks in the kitchen. Which is the curse, I think, of a lot of movies."

It seems that Barker is right, perhaps, to not complain about his Hollywood experiences. The 47-year-old British-born author and artist has accomplished a great deal since his career exploded in America. For one thing, he helped rescue the horror genre from the mire of silly slasher-killers dressed in sports equipment and made fright-fans remember that monsters can take many forms.

"I've actually been pretty lucky," he says. "*Hellraiser* is pretty much as I wanted it to be. The *Candyman* movies are pretty much as I wanted them to be. There is a director's cut of *Lord of Illusions* that is exactly as I want it to be. I've had wonderful people to work with and for. Even

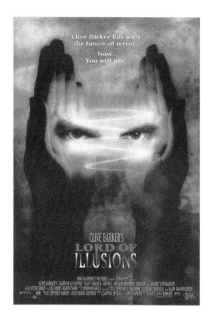

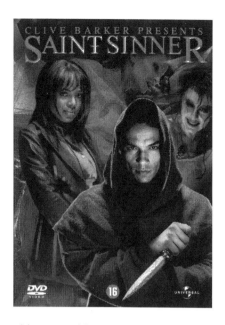

recently as *Gods and Monsters* we've had things that I'm very proud of up on screen. *Nightbreed* is the one that sort of fell between the stalls and was not protected. It was also my second movie and I just didn't know how to fight. And I didn't have a six-hundred pound gorilla to fight for me. And I lost that one.[1] [But] the fun thing is, each of these things is very different. The working processes to create those things are very different. So I find myself in a given week having both the solitary pleasures of going to my studio and painting or, as this afternoon, sitting and writing. But then I also have in a given week sitting down with writers who are taking my ideas and running with them in their own directions. It's very rewarding to be able to work with people who are as talented as these folks are. I think the town tends to be a bit too combative for its own good sometimes. There isn't enough attention paid to how collaborative all these processes really are. We are so caught up with the auteur theory, if you will, that we don't own up to the fact that movies are made by a lot of people, doing a lot of very different things. And hopefully all pulling in the same direction when they're doing it."

---

[1] *Note: Shout Factory's horror arm, Scream Factory, released the closest thing to a director's cut of **Nightbreed** we're likely to see. Inspired by the success of the "Cabal Cut"—a lengthy workprint version of the film that made the convention rounds in the early twenty-teens, the **Nightbreed Director's Cut** is head-and-shoulders above the long-lamented Theatrical Version and is highly recommended.*

For all of your up-to-date Clive Barker needs, please visit http://clivebarker.info/.

"I always wanted a character like Munkar," says actor Mary Mara. "A a role that a man would get in a movie. A Jack Nicholson kind of role. They don't write roles like this for women. They do on stage, but not really for television or film."

"Munkar" is one of a pair of female demons accidentally re-leased on our modern day world by a young monk in the nineteenth century. Her eternal partner is "Nakir", played by former child actress Rebecca Harrell (*Prancer*), and together, the duo is unleashing chaos, destruction and bloodshed across the Pacific Northwest, draining the life energies from every man they come across.

"Munkar"
Mary Mara

*Saint Sinner,* produced for the cable network by Oscar L. Costo (*Prancer Returns*), directed by Joshua Butler (*Good Vs. Evil*) and was adapted by Doris Egan (*Pleasantville*) from an original treatment by Clive Barker himself. As to be expected from a Barker tale, the demons bring with them much darkness and horror. Still, Mara and Harrell don't see themselves as the "sinner" part of the title.

"Whenever you play a villain, you can never make a negative judgment about the character you're playing. There's nowhere to go with 'no'," Mara says. "You definitely don't make a judgment about these char-acters, good or evil. Josh calls us the heroes all the time. When he's setting up a shot, he'll call it a 'hero shot', and I really love that. We're the heroes! We have to kill these people because we have to sustain our lives. It's not murder, it's not a sin, it's just what we have to do to sustain our life. So it's pretty simple."

That the actors don't make judgments is an interesting choice, as it echoes the choices Barker himself has made in his fiction. Rarely does he present his characters as "good" or "evil" inherently, though they are often defined as one or the other through their ultimate actions. "For [Rebecca and me], it's all about the relationship between Munkar and Nakir. [There are] many, many, many levels. Mother-daughter. Protector. Hunter. Lover. Sister. It's more a human—it's a nonsexual relationship, if that's at all possible in a way. We just take on these bodies because we're in this world at this moment. Our energy takes on these two female bodies. So I choose to believe that if we were to go into another time or another wormhole, we would take on whatever physical body everyone else had. So it just happens this time that we're women. It could be expressed as a lover's relationship, or a maternal relationship. I think in our relationship, I am always the teacher and she is always the student."

The multi-leveled relationship was a difficult one to develop, thanks to the nature of television productions. Mara and Harrell had little time together in pre-production. "We got here a week before shooting started. It was a lot of costume fittings, and everybody has been off in their separate places, thinking about their characters, then they come together 'okay, here's my idea'. Then, there's the costumes, the make-up, what about the hair? And you're trying to develop the look of the characters, the look of the team, and still find your own way. That's a very exciting part of it. I think the real stuff going on is that I'm older, she's younger. We've both been in the business a long time [yet] I've been through a lot more experience than her. It's been really an interesting time. God, it would have been a great documentary. She had brought up a few times that [the situations] didn't feel organic. You're in these kind of elevated situations, and I think what we've been finding is the theatrics of it are what hook you in. It's easy to identify with anything if you just believe. I joke that she's not the same person that showed up four weeks ago from L.A. She's not. She's grown a lot! She's a lot tougher. This is not an easy role and last week we were covered in mud and filth and dust and goo and KY and we're fighting and slamming each other into walls. You know, there are a lot of actresses who wouldn't want to do that. And wouldn't do it. But she and I are completely gung-ho, and we went much further than anyone expected. Of course, no one expected us to do most of our stunts. We were able to do pretty much all of them."

Mara, of course, is no stranger to action or dark fantasy, thanks to previous television experiences. She had an impressive role on an early episode of the cult favorite *Farscape* ("I was one of the only Americans they ever flew in," she says), and enjoyed a recurring role on the Don Johnson cop series, *Nash Bridges*. "We pretty much blew things up and shot things [on *Nash*]. Endlessly," she says with a laugh. "I was always begging the stunt co-ordinator for stunts. He always liked me and joked that if I ever retired, he'd train me as a stunt person. That's like being a kid and getting to climb a tree. It's a great job for a woman. They get to do stuff that women just don't get to do—and there's no reason [they shouldn't]. We have really wonderful women up here too."

It's a common complaint among working actresses: the lack of solid work for women in Hollywood. Thanks to shows like *Buffy the*

*Photo courtesy Mary Mara.*

*Vampire Slayer* and *Alias*, women are being called upon to both emote and fight more and more often. "Kick ass" females are popular right now. Mara sees this as a very good thing, but could stand to happen even more.

"This female action role in an hour-long televison show is a good coup. Television has always been a female medium; the majority of people who watch TV are women. So there are really good roles for women on television. I think it's still a very youth-oriented culture. The action roles are good, though. Nobody wants to take the sexuality away from women. I know a lot of men and women who [have similar personalities]. It's not about sexuality anymore. The tomboy in us all. It's such a sense of play too."

*All **Saint Sinner** photos copyright Seraphim Films. All Rights Reserved.*

*Saint Sinner* has been a playful challenge, as well, it seems. Munkar and Nakir should prove to be memorable villains, thanks to the well-drawn roles as well as the elaborate make-up courtesy of artist Mike Fields. As is often the case with prosthetics, the accent is on visual feast rather than personal comfort. Mara and Harrell get the additional challenge of playing characters who are often covered with slime. "It's not so bad because it's not cold. I think if it were cold it would be a lot worse. Plus, the guy who is doing our make-up, Mike Fields is a total horror fanatic. Knows everything about it. Couldn't be the better person to be doing our make-up and taking care of us and putting goo on us all day. Rebecca and I don't know that much about it. He's got horror flicks running on the TV in the makeup trailer all day. Working with prosthetics and special effects, it's all about relaxation. That was the mantra I kept repeating to Rebecca yesterday [during a big elaborate special-effects scene]. Because it takes so much time patience is definitely a must. I've been on a lot of sets and I know how sets work. It's not that complex. But people sometimes forget that it's an enormous group effort and a lot of patience is involved. They were rushing us through in the morning, seven or eight o'clock, and we worked all day. Then we didn't actually cover me until 8:00 at night. All day long, we covered her, camera-wise, and then at the end of the night, they turned around and covered me. That's an interesting process to go through. You're acting the intensity of the scene but the camera isn't on you."

(Which speaks acres about Mara's professionalism. How many times have you heard about the big-time actor who went to his trailer rather than stand opposite his co-star and act while the other was in close-up? "Oh, god, that's so obnoxious," says Mara. "I just want to slap people like that. You have one of the greatest jobs in the world, and you're being paid more money than people should have, what's the big deal? I have a problem with those actors that, all of a sudden there are things they just can't do. Just stop it!" But the question is, what attracted Mara to the role of the ancient demon? For this author, Mara is best known as the gold-digging woman who mis-used the title elixir in the Sandra Bullock vehicle *Love Potion No. 9*, and winds up running down the streets of San Francisco, pursued by a hoard of love-struck men. What would prompt an actress to take on a potentially unsympathetic role that has multiple strikes against it just from a genre point of view. Unless handled in exactly the right way, the demons could become over-blown and campy cartoons, the horror falling flat under over-wrought production.

"Clive Barker, for one," she says. "His work is just terrific. I love sci-fi, I love Sci-Fi channel. I love the subject matter, and I'd never done a horror movie. Clive started in theater, and when I see [a horror movie like his] I think that looks like 'Medea or 'Electra' or something like that. Some fabulous Greek tragedy! When acting in most television in America, you only use a tiny bit of your talent. You don't have to use a lot of muscle, because the medium is small. The parts are not that demanding. The most demanding thing is if you have to cry all the time. People always hire me to cry. I get so sick of that. There is so much else I can do, come on! Saint Sinner is more theatrical than anything I've done, other than stage, obviously. And that's what is so great about it, it's such food. Rebecca and I keep commenting about, the days just fly by. It's seven-thirty at night, we're going 'holey moley!' We've gone through this amazing huge experience. There's so much about television and film that is about making the actor smaller. You have to make yourself smaller. The medium is smaller. And

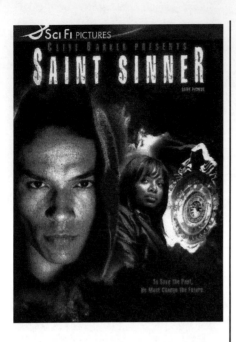

it's so nice to be able to go bigger, larger with a character. There's something very invigorating and empowering about that.

It's like Willem DaFoe in *Spider Man*. I love him! He's so great. The scene where he talks to himself in the mirror. He was wonderful. Growling. It was so cool. Guys get to play those roles all the time. So it's nice to be given the opportunity to do that, as a woman. The only other way I can see where I would be given that opportunity is to go back to the theater."

Mara hopes that *Saint Sinner* will strike a chord with audiences not just to forge new opportunities for her, but for actresses in general. "I'd like to see more female fantasy-driven films. Female sci-fi driven work. There are a lot of wonderful women writing sci-fi. They've been scooping up every sci-fi book they can find to make into a movie recently, ever since *Lord of the Rings*, all these very obscure ones.

"I have a dream project that we adapted into a screenplay for Sci-Fi. I don't want to give anything away right now, but it's a cross between *Animal Farm* and *Raiders Of The Lost Ark*. It's fantastic. If I was a well-connected person, I could probably get it green-lighted easily. It has all the goods. But it's hard when you're not with CAA or ICM. So it comes down to trying to get to people who can get to people. I couldn't have picked a small project!" [laughs]

As for the movie itself, it has the potential to move beyond its ninety-minute running time. Barker's ideas tend to expand beyond themselves, into unexpected directions. Saint Sinner is no exception and Mara recognizes that potential. "I would love for this thing to turn into a series, and I'd get to direct. That's what I'd love. What famous female monsters can you name? Besides the *Bride Of Frankenstein*. It all depends on if there's a demand. Lord willing we're going to hit a nerve. We're taking a huge risk, and hopefully it will pay off for us."

Following *Saint Sinner*, Mara took roles in an astonishing number of cult TV shows, including *Bones, Dexter, Shameless,* and the films *Gridiron Gang* and *Prom Night.*

Boy. When some people look to change their image, they don't fool around. Rebecca Harrell is probably best known as the little girl in *Prancer*, who discovers Santa's reindeer in her back yard. In Clive Barker's Saint Sinner, a new movie being produced for the Sci-Fi Channel, Harrell stars as "Nakir", one of a pair of slime-oozing female demons who must drain the life-forces from men to survive. *Prancer*: good little girl, eats her vegetables, loves father Sam Elliot. *Saint Sinner*: other-worldly ancient crea-ture, eats humans, loves her mentor/ partner/lover Munkar (Mary Mara). Image successfully changed.

"Nakir"
Rebecca Harrell

"I really liked the idea of playing something other than the 'mousey good girl'," Harrell tells me, via phone from her Vancouver hotel room. Filming on Saint Sinner is continuing, but this is the first break Harrell has had in over a week. "You get type-cast into things. I've always been "the *Prancer* girl". It's amazing to me that they're still running *Prancer* every week on television. Even now in the middle of summer, they're running *Prancer* out of season. It's pretty amazing. And then in October you're going to be able to turn to Sci-Fi and see me very post-pubescent [laughs]. I'll always be "the *Prancer* girl". That sort of follows me

around, and it will probably for the rest of my life. People look at my resume and go 'oh, yeah, *Prancer*'. [But] we all have to transcend to our adult careers at some time. I really got down and dirty in that audition. I really wanted this job. I got down on the floor, and I was rolling around, and I really wanted to show that I could play something other than innocent and sweet. In making this trans-formation into this adult world. I'm still a young woman, and I wanted to show that I have another side to myself that's not sweet. I used all of my sexual energy and I just shot it out right at them, through my body language. And [director Joshua Butler] said that that's really what got me the job, the body language. I'm very physical. I could use my body to explain [the story] along with the dialogue. He said that's a gift that I have."

As illustrated, Nakir is as far from her character in *Prancer* as you can get. Nakir isn't even human. She and Munkar are timeless beings, imprisoned for centuries inside a mystical orb that protects mankind from their ravenous appetites. "I came up with this whole elaborate story for myself about how she was formed. Basically she's been sucking the blood and souls of men to survive. They've destroyed cities and civilizations of people. They're a whole different breed. Munkar and I are partners in crime throughout the centuries. I'm the "lure", I'm the trap. I basically lure the men in with sex and then we both devour them."

Harrell finishes the description with a laugh that is almost a giggle, proving that there's still a little girl deep inside her. Nakir probably ate her. While the desire to move into adult roles has been a priority with Harrell for some time, there wasn't much appeal to going the Elizabeth Berkeley *Showgirls* route for the former "*Prancer* girl".

"My favorite actress is Cate Blanchett," Harrell says. "And the reason [is] that she absolutely morphs herself into different people for whatever that role is. Everybody brings a little bit of themselves into every role, but she makes herself, as Cate Blanchett, almost unrecognizable. That is truly acting, being able to truly morph yourself into someone else, [and] that's what I'm trying to do with this role. Nakir is certainly not me, and it's a huge

challenge. It's one of the biggest acting challenges I've ever been faced with. There's not a lot of myself I can bring to this role. I just thought, 'what an opportunity!' I love to shock people. I thought, what a great reel I'm going to have when this is over. I'm going to have me as a nine-year-old girl, Sam Elliot's daughter, then you'll have me being the monster. That's what attracted me to this role."

*Saint Sinner* isn't Harrell's first foray into horror—the honors go to the respected but little seen *Suspended Animation* for that—this is her first opportunity to play the monster. Because it's a character created by Clive Barker, Nakir is a character that allowed Harrell to really stretch her talents to bring Nakir to life. "I came up for this whole background for why [Nakir does what she does]—of course, it's not going to be given away in this movie. There are so many interesting directions we could go in this movie and we're basically only touching on this. And how fun to get to play a demon. Of course, I don't think of myself of a demon. In terms of acting, I don't think that's a very interesting choice, because then, through-out the movie, you're just playing at being evil. I think what makes a demon a really wonderful character is when they think what they're doing is the right thing. Then they have just cause and they're fighting for something

*Sam Elliott, Harrell, and the title character in Prancer.*

too." Harrell continues, "My character is very animalistic. In nature, a creature that's luring their prey, eating other animals, doesn't think of itself as doing anything wrong. They think of themselves as survival. That's what it is for me. Killing and eating these men isn't being evil, it's all about sustenance and wanting to breed and wanting to help my gene pool to continue and perhaps take over. That's what we've been trying to do for centuries. There is a very, very strong relationship between Munkar and I. We're the only kind of these demons, and there is a very interesting, very dark, long history. It's almost as if we're playing *Romeo and Juliet* in a sense. Even though we're two women, we really wanted to take this to the edge. We've really wanted to turn these two women into something that had never been done before. So we have made really interesting choices, I think. From the script, you can turn it into many different things from the dialogue, but it's the subtext. I think that she and I have really developed an interesting relationship in this movie that people are going to want to watch. Even though we're sucking blood from the men, and doing all these horrible things, I think we can get people to feel compassionate towards us. People are going to want to see more of us, even though we're doing these terrible things.

And that was my goal. I, myself, am a pacifist. I'm all for doing good in the world. I had this ideal that I was only going to do movies that made people leave the theater and want to do good in the world. Hopefully, there is that message in this movie, but there are also other messages in it as well. [laughs] I'm not necessarily representing the good. I'm representing the despicable in a sense."

"Good" is represented by Greg Serano and Gina Ravera, playing Brother Tomas and Detective Dressler, respectively. The former is a nineteenth century monk who travels through time pursuing the demons— which is only fair, seeing as how he causes the accident that releases them. Ravera's Dressler is a modern day cop who doesn't really buy into the spiritual aspect of the mission, but

recognizes the two women as a force that has to be stopped. Terrible things happen throughout the movie, mostly at the hands of the demons. Violence plays a large part in Saint Sinner, and the Sci-Fi Channel is rising to the challenge of not looking away when the horror happens. That was a challenge for Harrell as well.

"Before I came up here I did some homework. I watched *Lord of Illusions* and *Hellraiser*, and it was hard for me at first because horror and sci-fi are not my genres in movies. They're not the kinds of movies I would even sit down and watch. I'm a very sensitive person and they actually disturb me. I pick up on that energy and that sets my mood for that day. So, I watched *Lord of Illusions* with Clive's commentary, and he finds it all so amusing. Because it is so disturbing you have to be able to laugh. I had to take that into account when I was looking into my role. I figured that I had to have a sense of humor about it [and then] Nakir would have a sense of humor about it. So I've really incorporated that into it—things make me laugh, things make me happy. Very animalistic on the one hand, and very childlike on the other hand. Things surprise her. This is the first time she's ever been in modern society. One of the first scenes I have is me watching television and absorbing the energy from the television. Of course, I've been raised with television, but I had to approach the scene as if I was seeing the television for the first time. What an interesting concept that is. I had to really sit down and think about it before we did the scene. How would I respond to all of these things that we've created for ourselves in this modern day society if we'd never seen anything like them before? And it almost makes me feel that we are here to reclaim [the Earth]. I'm a firm believer that nature will always win— this is the sort of positive spin on my character. Here [humans have] built cities and destroyed the earth, so in my mind, we're almost the heroes! We're coming to do a little population control. [laughs] [Nakir and Munkar talk] about humans breeding and spreading, the children are ravenous and want to consume, consume, consume! 'There are tons of food bags walking around and making noise!' You know? So what's the problem? There is so much to consume, because there's an overpopulation of people, here we are to balance out the world again."

"Fortunately for us, you know, you can't kill us," Harrell says, again with a laugh. "We're very symbolic, these two demons. We're trying not to make ourselves symbols for women. Even though we are in the form of two women and we're sucking the blood of men, I would like to think of myself in a broad spectrum of behavior, not so much of women. Then I don't feel that I'd be representing myself well. I'm not being true to myself in portraying the character in this way. Instead I feel it's lust, it's temptation—I represent temptation, and greed, I know this is a strange word, but naivete in a sense, my character with Munkar."

In order to avoid making Nakir a cliché—your average villainous bitch seen in hundreds of low-budget gore-fests—Harrell worked hard to bring all these symbolic aspects to Nakir. While much of the "demonic" aspect will be taken care of through the make-up provided by the Tatopoulos Company, both Mara and Harrell had to "work through the prosthetics" and reveal the characters beneath. "I studied my cat, Bonnie, for this role before I came out here to Vancouver. I have a Siamese Cat, and I watched her and how she reacted and responded to things. And animals are kind of naïve in a sense. Animals don't so much plan things, they can't hold more than one thought at a time. They're in survival mode, always. Bonnie has her cat food and her litter box, of course, so it isn't like she's out hunting for things. But she'll listen to something, and she'll get bothered by it and whip her tail around. When she'd play with my dog, I'd watch how she'd pounce and how she would sit and watch and wait and prowl, and that's what I wanted to turn this character into. [As a result] I'm not pre-planning anything. I know my lines, but I'm not making my choices until I get onto the set. Like my cat, I want to react to what is going on around me. It all affects me. It's like sensory overload. I'll accentuate my spine movement, the way a cat will arch it's back and respond. You can tell what a cat is thinking through its body language. And I wanted it to be the same for me with this character. We're in human form, but we're not human. Josh has given me absolute freedom with this character. I basically experiment with every single take. He definitely has guided me and sent Mary and I onto our own direction. But it's such an interesting process because neither Mary nor I know what we're going to do before we get onto the set! [laughs] We just go and do it. I truly believe that the best choice in handling these characters is that they respond to what's in front of them, and they make decisions based on that, the way an animal would. Unlike humans, who spend all day thinking about what's going to happen tomorrow, and what happened yesterday, an animal is only

able to be present in the moment. And that's how I'm working in these scenes. I've never played anything like this before! I've always played sweet and kind and giving and loving, I've never been able to play the demon."

The challenges weren't just emotional and psychological. Saint Sinner is a character-driven film, but that doesn't mean that the film is skimping on the special effects. Soho Visual Effects studio provides the CGI, and the rest is handled by Tatopoulos [which also includes work by Friends of E.N. Gabe Bartalos and John P. Fedele]. That means the majority of the special effects are practical: puppets, stage magic and make-up. "For the most part, we're just air-brushed. We sit in make-up for an hour and they cover our skin with an airbrush. For certain scenes in the movie, I become more demonic, and I wear a full prosthetic chest. It's sort of an obstacle in a sense to focus on what I'm supposed to be focusing on in the scene. And they goo us every day with this K-Y Jelly! Goo! Goo, everywhere! That's Josh's famous line from this movie: 'More goo!' The goo is just the icing to the cake. Working with the prosthetics, working with the goo, working within these unreal circumstances, how do you make it real? How do you work through the goo?"

There is also plenty of action in *Saint Sinner*, something that Harrell wasn't precisely prepared for, but didn't shy away from getting down and dirty in the fight scenes. "And thank god! [laughs] This role requires a great deal of physical activity. I've never done stunts like this in my entire life. Beating people up, driving people through beams, just kicking and punching and fighting. I've done

THE TRUTH

IS DEEP BENEATH

THE SURFACE

THE BIGFIX

OFFICIAL SELECTION

BEACH OPEN

all but two of my own stunts. And belive me there have been a lot of stunts. But Mary and I really wanted to step up to the plate on this. I didn't even know I had it in me to be honest. I thought that a stunt double would end up doing most of the stunts. As it turns out, what a wonderful surprise, I would love to do more physical stuff in movies! It's that adrenaline! I've never hit anyone in my life. We don't really hit each other, but there were times when I would be working with Munkar's stunt double [Crystal Dalman] or Mary would be working with mine [Leanne Buchanan], for the stuff where there was no way around it. Munkar and I get into this huge fight, a couple of times [laughs]. [At one point] I force her through these

huge beams while they break away. I'd never done anything like this before. You get on the set and everyone wants to get the shot, the sun is starting to go down—but I stepped up to the plate. There were some problems—the ground was very muddy, I'm wearing these ridiculous shoes! We did it two times and both times, two of the boards wouldn't break. So here I am, driving this poor woman through these boards—I'm pushing, she's choking and they're not breaking. But that was what the shot was. That's what she was getting paid to do, for me though, it was very hard. I don't want to hurt anybody. She was so sweet and wonderful about it 'no, it was great, you did a great job!' The adrenaline is just pumping! It was really amazing and it made me feel really, really strong. Even though I couldn't walk on Saturday. I was covered head to toe in bruises, my side was all scraped. But you know, I loved it! I was so proud of myself. It made me feel like I could do anything. I didn't think I had that in me. Screw therapy, I'm just going to become a stunt woman!"

In the years following *Saint Sinner,* Harrell has turned her attention towards environmental activism. She wrote a book, "Hot, Rich and Green: The Secret Formula Women are Using to Get Rich and Save the Planet", and with her husband, Josh Tickell, wrote, produced and directed the films *The Big Fix* (2010) about the BP Oil Spill disaster in the Gulf of Mexico, and *Pump* (2014) about about ending America's dependence on oil. The couple's official website is https://www.bigpictureranch.com/

# THE ENLIGHTENED HEATHEN: A FOLK HORROR PRIMER
## by William Wright

If you're a horror fan and keep up with the genre press to any extent, you may have noticed the term folk horror, or, more specifically, British folk horror, cropping up in your news feed quite a bit over the last year or so thanks largely to the critical success of Robert Eggers 2015 supernatural sleeper hit, *The Witch*. Situated in a nebulous area that is not quite sub-genre, e.g., vampires or zombies, nor specifically a synthesis of genres like science fiction horror, e.g., *Alien, Event Horizon*. Owing to its narrative malleability, horror has long defied the strident application of convention in contrast to the structural formalism of other genres such as the Western, therefore it is perhaps best to approach the folk horror phenomenon as, to borrow the vocabulary of music theory, a *mode* within the larger framework the genre.

The term "folk horror" came into popular usage thanks to British writer, producer, actor and lifelong horrorphile Mark Gatiss (*Sherlock, Doctor Who*) who uses it to describe a specific, albeit brief, late/post Hammer Film Productions break with Gothicism in British horror film in the late 1960s and early '70s characterized by themes of folklore, paganism, witchcraft and the supernatural in his essential 2010 BBC Television documentary series *A History of Horror*. The initial wave of folk horror is distinctly a product of its era in its dark, post-Summer of Love obsessions. As the idealism of flower power was choked by the weeds of an unending, unpopular war, campus violence, assassination and a drug culture that delivered addiction and poverty instead of the enlightenment it promised, an undeniably uneasy feeling that the hippie ethos of peace and love had gone rancid—a feeling cemented by the Manson Family and the 1969 Tate-La Bianca murders. "Leave a sign... Something witchy," cult leader Charles Manson had admonished his family of young, disenfranchised killers before sending them on their gruesome mission to Cielo Drive simultaneously fore-shadowing and igniting a spark of occult paranoia which would affect Western culture for decades to come. As the 1970s dawned, it seemed to many that both the traditional institutions of civilization and the counterculture had failed. Springing forth from this malaise was a resurgence in mainstream interest in all things paranormal and occult of a magnitude not seen since the Victorian era and the rise of Spiritualism. The occult became both method and madness, curative and scapegoat -- a way of coping with and placing blame for the evils of a rapidly evolving world. In a stroke of divine irony, pop culture and film mined the superstitions of the Western European, pre-Christian, pagan past just as man set foot on the moon, and although Neil Armstrong may have strode across the forehead of the Goddess Luna, the Horned God held sway on the earth below.

Allegorical and thematic baggage aside, the plot of the archetypal folk horror film often adheres to a specific pattern and series of motifs: the setting is isolated and generally rural; there is nearly always an insular if not outwardly secretive community; the narrative begins with a mysterious inciting incident such as a murder, a disappearance or some other inexplicable and possibly supernatural event; an outsider or outsiders (either benign or malevolent) arrive to seek a resolution and otherwise disrupt the status quo; the outsider(s) is either

*Vincent Price as Witchfinder General Matthew Hopkins in **The Conqueror Worm**. Photo copyright American International Pictures.*

triumphant or destroyed physically, morally or spiritually.

Gatiss cites three films as the foundation of the folk horror style, all of which adhere to the aforementioned blueprint to varying degrees: *Witchfinder General* (Michael Reeves, 1968), *The Blood on Satan's Claw* (Piers Haggard, 1971) and *The Wicker Man* (Robin Hardy, 1973) The sum of these three films has come to equal the paradigm of the folk horror style. Known to fans and scholars alike as "the unholy trinity" these films are ground zero for any introductory study of the style.

Michael Reeves' *Witchfinder General*, released in the United States as *The Conqueror Worm* and deceptively promoted as an Edgar Allan Poe tale to cash in on distributor American International Pictures' wildly successful run of loose adaptations of the author's work and their star Vincent Price, is the grimmest and most brutal of folk horror's "unholy trinity." Ostensibly based in fact, *Witchfinder General* is set during the English Civil War of the 17th century. Price portrays Matthew Hopkins, a corrupt and brutal self-styled witch hunter with an alleged mandate to snuff out witchcraft and sorcery in the English countryside. An opportunist and unremitting villain, Hopkins exploits the chaos of the conflict between the Royalist and Parliamentary forces to line his pockets and indulge his more prurient instincts in the name of the Church and at the expense of the innocent. When John Lowes (Rupert Davies), a village priest, runs afoul of Hopkins, his niece Sara (Hilary Dwyer), betrothed to Richard Marshall (Ian Ogilvy), a young Roundhead soldier, offers herself to

the witch finder in exchange for her uncle's life. An incensed Marshall soon returns swearing vengeance upon Hopkins and his henchman, Stearne (Robert Russell) in a bloody pursuit to rival his enemies' own reign of terror. Witchfinder General is a remarkably brutal and violent film even by 21st century standards. Its graphic depiction of torture juxtaposed with its bucolic English country setting retains its power to shock nearly fifty years after its release. Vincent Price gives one of his very best genre performances eschewing the broad villainy and over-the-top campiness that marks much of his AIP era work for restrained menace, subtlety and genuine depth.

Price's clashes with the wunderkind director Reeves have become the stuff of legend (Reeves apparently wanted Donald Pleasence for Hopkins and made no secret of it to either the crew or Price himself, but co-financier AIP insisted on Price as a guaranteed box office draw). Sadly, Witchfinder General would be Reeves final film. Suffering from depression and insomnia, the twenty-five year-old filmmaker died of an accidental overdose of alcohol and barbiturates just nine mon ths after the film's release.

By all conventional cinematic wisdom, a film with a title as sensational as The Blood on Satan's Claw should be on the second tier of a drive-in double feature. Nevertheless, cliche´ warns us of books and their covers and that threadbare adage can, in this case, also be applied to a movie and its title. Piers Haggard's 1971 demonic thriller is one of the best British horror films of the 1970s. A mere synopsis of The Blood on Satan's Claw does no justice to the film's quality or impact. If anything, on paper, the plot as described only reinforces the inherent corniness of the title. So, be forewarned and undeterred—what follows must be experienced, preferably in the dark. Like Witchfinder General, The Blood on Satan's Claw has a pastoral, historical setting, this time an isolated village in the early 18th century. A young farmer named Ralph Gower (Barry Andrews) unleashes a demonic curse when he tills up a bizarre, malformed skull with a single cloudy, blue eye while plowing his field.

Panicked and fearful, Gower pleads with an incredulous visiting judge (veteran actor Patrick Wymark in his penultimate role) to examine the grotesque remains. Naturally, the skull has vanished and the judge dismisses Gower's claims as simple, unenlightened superstition. Soon after, a series of inexplicable, super-natural events befall the community many centering on the village's children who begin growing patches of coarse fur on their bodies. The children also seem to have fallen under the diabolical influence of the devilish (and demonically possessed) vixen Angel Blake (Linda Hayden). It soon becomes apparent that an ancient malevolent force intends to physically manifest by growing itself piecemeal on the flesh of the innocent. At last, the judge returns to confront the ancient evil head on, now pragmatically armed with a new found knowledge of witchcraft and the occult.

*The Blood on Satan's Claw* was initially conceived as something of a spiritual successor to *Witchfinder General*. Commissioned by Chilton Films, a company formed by producers Peter Andrews and Malcolm Heyward, writer Robert Wynne-Simmons (*The Outcasts*, 1982) was instructed to include several key elements from the 1968 Vincent Price vehicle including the *Book of Witches* and a trial-by-drowning sequence. Originally, the film was to be an Amicus style portmanteau of three loosely connected witchcraft tales book ended with a framing story. Although this format was abandoned early on, the final film still bears the marks of its episodic origins. Nevertheless, it never becomes disjointed thanks to director Piers Haggard's directorial skill and focus on character building. In spite of its historical setting, the horror of *The Blood on Satan's Claw* is firmly rooted in the late 1960s.

*Girl's Mayday out on Summersisle from* **The Wicker Man**. *Photo copyright British Lion Films*

Wynne-Simmons has cited the combined influence of the infamous case of Mary Bell, an 11 year-old Newcastle girl who strangled and mutilated two small boys in 1968, and the Manson cult as the impetus of the film's narrative. In *A History Horror,* Director Haggard further elaborated on the tumultuous era's rule bending influence: "...I think I was trying to make a folk horror film in a way because we were all a bit interested in witchcraft; we were all a bit interested in free love. The rules of the cinema were changing and nudity became possible (and) indeed, possibly over-prevalent because the lid had been slightly taken off."

Haggard also outlines the film's most disturbing scene, a brutal, ritual rape in a ruined church, as an oblique metaphor for the times: "...It's about a complete breakdown of our values. A very beautiful procession coming to the church chanting in the blossoms turns into something very ugly, and the beautiful boughs are used as scourges and whips. If I look at the rape scene now, I think it's probably too strong, and it's interesting that I wasn't bothered at the time..."

The third film of folk horror's unholy trinity was once hailed in the pages of *Cinefantastique* as "the *Citizen Kane* of horror film" and occupies *The Guardian*'s list of the 25 best horror films at number four above Nosferatu, *The Exorcist* and *The Bride of Frankenstein*. Hyperbole and accolades aside, Robin Hardy's *The Wicker Man* (1973) is a thriller like no other before or after it. Largely devoid of violence and cheap scares, it is absolutely bloodless relying not on pulse-pounding suspense, but a slowly unfolding plot punctuated by an absolute hammer blow of an ending. Utterly mesmerizing in execution, *The Wicker Man* manages to sincerely

touch something of the pagan and the primitive in its audience drawing us in on gossamer threads of natural beauty and music to identify not with the supposed "hero" but with his heathen and hedonistic foes. If this one doesn't make you want to dance naked among the standing stones, check your pulse; you may be dead inside. *The Wicker Man* breaks with the period trappings of *Witchfinder General* and *The Blood on Satan's Claw* opting for a contemporary setting. The plot is, at least in the opening moments of the film, a deceptively standard mystery. Having received an anonymous letter, upright, up tight and upstanding police Sergeant Howie (Edward Woodward) lands on the secluded Hebridean island of Summerisle in search of clues in the disappearance of a local girl named Rowan Morrison (Geraldine Cowper). The pious Howie is shocked to find that the provincial islanders have seemingly regressed to their pagan roots, abandoning Christianity to worship the Celtic gods of fertility and harvest. Howie's puritanical attitudes are met with obstruction from the locals at every turn and clues to the whereabouts of the young girl lead to one dead end after another. Having at last found what he assumes is Rowan Morrison's grave in a "defiled" cemetery, Howie meets with the island's namesake and de facto governor Lord Summerisle (Christopher Lee) who explains how his grandfather, a Victorian agronomist who developed strains of fruit that could survive in the harsh climes of the Scottish coast encouraged the population to return to the worship the old gods who would bring prosperity to the island. At last, Howie comes to the conclusion that Rowan is indeed alive and is to be offered as a human sacrifice following a failed harvest. In the end, Howie discovers too late the nature of the islanders' conspiracy: Rowan has been used as willing bait in a trap to snare the sergeant himself as the ultimate sacrifice. Meeting his fiery fate in a towering, man-shaped sacrificial pyre, Howie raises his voice to sing "Psalm 23 (The Lord is my Shepherd)" only to be drowned out by the crackling of flames and the islanders own rousing rendition of the old English folk tune "Sumer Is Icumen In."

By the early 1970s, Christopher Lee already an icon of the horror genre for more than decade had become weary of his typecasting in Hammer's seemingly endless series of initially ground-breaking, but by the end of the 1960s rather long-in-the-tooth, Dracula films. Looking for a challenge up to his formidable acting skills, Lee partnered with screenwriter Anthony Schaffer who had written Alfred Hitchcock's late career hit, *Frenzy* (1972) and the Academy

*Christopher Lee as Lord Summerisle in* **The Wicker Man.**
*Photo copyright British Lion Films*

Award-nominated thriller *Sleuth* (1972) in hopes of developing a suitable project. Producer Peter Snell and director Robin Hardy were soon brought into the fold. Shaffer and Hardy, both longtime fans of horror, consciously rejected the baroque Hammer style to focus on something they found compelling and seldom seen: a different, "more literate" horror film rooted in the "old religion" of Western European paganism rather than in Victorian potboilers. Shaffer explains the

detective story..." Although it is now considered a classic, *The Wicker Man* had a notoriously troubled distribution. Near the film's completion, studio British Lion headed by Snell was acquired by EMI who frankly had no idea how to handle the film. It was subsequently cut (and re-cut) and unceremoniously released at the bottom of a double bill —in a time when double bills were already an anachronism—with the equally problematic and also undeniably brilliant *Don't Look Now*.

genesis of the film in David Gregory's 2001 video documentary *The Wicker Man Enigma*: "I had for quite a feasible amount of time wanted to do a film in the, for want of a better word, horror movie genre without it actually following in the rather tired footsteps of Hammer Films...And it occurred to me that I had never actually seen a film on the nature of sacrifice. It seemed to me, also, that I ought to try and dress it up in a way as that provided something in the shock

In retrospect, it seems that the only film distributor with any inkling of how to handle the film was legendary low-budget master marketer Roger Corman who was unfortunately outbid for U.S. rights. In *The Wicker Man Enigma,* Corman relates, "We were distributing for Bergman, Fellini, Truffaut, a number of European directors, and I saw this picture as something that would be somewhere between an art film and a

commercial film. On one one level, it was a fantasy film with a little bit of horror; on another level, it was more intelligent than most of that type of film and could be sold not necessarily as an art film but as sort of an upper bracket film vaguely in that genre." Echoing Corman's sentiments, *The Wicker Man* continues to represent an intellectual divide within and between fandom and the critical community.

*The Wicker Man* stands as that rare horror film that is subversive even within the context of an admittedly subversive genre. From the deceptive casting of such staples of British horror as Christopher Lee and Ingrid Pitt to its protagonist who is so loathsome in his piety that he inspires the audience to identify with Summerisle's "villainous" pagans, *The Wicker Man* defies simple categorization within the confines of genre. Yes, it is horrific and shocking as any worthy horror film should be,

but it is also beautiful, compelling and ultimately haunting. A word of caution: *The Wicker Man* was needlessly remade in 2006 starring Nicolas Cage. It is to be avoided like the plague.

In conclusion, if you are looking for break from the endless deluge of post-Romero zom-bie fare and rehashed 1980s slashers or you simply like your horror with a little more intellectual and stylistic heft, I suggest you seek out these three films before diving headlong into the current folk horror revival. If you find you enjoy the style, and I find it quite addictive, your next stop should be the Folk Horror website at **FolkHorror.com** for a comprehensive listing of folk horror in literature, film and TV. Of the recent crop of folk horror revival films, I would definitely suggest *The Witch*. Watch it with an open mind and try to ignore both the hype and the backlash. It's effective and simultaneously frightening and heart-breaking. However, if your tastes lean toward the artistic and the surreal, I cannot recommend Ben Wheatley's *A Field in England* enough. It is a black-and-white, psyche-delic nightmare set, much like *Witchfinder General*, during the English Civil War focusing on a mad alchemist and a band of captured battlefield deserters searching for a buried treasure. If you enjoy the work of Luis Buñuel or David Lynch, this film is not to be missed.

Until next time, live deliciously.

# VAMPIRES DON'T HAVE TAN LINES

## BY MIKE WATT

As long as there have been vampires, there have been lesbian vampires. Or so I'm told by the countless low-budget sex & blood fests that line the shelves of video stores across America.

The idea of the lesbian vampire is not a new one, of course. If one is intrepid enough to investigate the vampire legend, you can go as far back as Lilith, rumored to be Adam's first wife and the world's first vampire according to the Kaballah, who one night seduced both Adam and his new wife Eve.

The basis of the lesbian vampire tale has its roots in J. Sheridan Le Fanu's 1872 novel, *Carmilla*, itself in turn based on the legends of 17th century Hungarian noblewoman and famed serial killer, Countess Elizabeth

Báthory de Ecsed. Predating Bram Stoker's *Dracula* by 26 year, *Carmilla* spins its own web of Sapphic vampirism and repressed sensuality, upping an ante that Stoker's tale of blood and thunder can barely touch. Stoker's Dracula, of course, was a lusty heterosexual. Countess Carmilla (or Mircalla) Karnstein also prefers female blood. *Carmilla* gave birth to countless cinematic adaptations and distractions (see reviews to follow.) But in the mid-nineties, it was decided that a good way to make back the buck-seventy-five invested in a shot-on-video horror movie was to get a couple of sexy(ish) babes, jam a fifty-cent pair of plastic choppers in their mouths and let them writhe around for a while. Preferably naked and on top of each other. Honestly, with a winning formula like that, how can you possibly go wrong? Some of these movies have other things going for them aside from the flesh pressing. Most, however, don't. Most even end as soon as the final bite is delivered to whatever fleshy part is most available. These awe-inspiring events can be witnessed in such immortal classics as *Caress of the Vampire, The Vampire Strangler, Blood Kiss, Vampires of Sorority Row, Sorority House Vampires, Vampires in the Sorority House, House of the Sorority Vampires, There are Vampires in the Sorority House 2: The Electric Boogaloo,* and my personal favorite *The Vampire's Seduction* (in which topless vamp Tina Krause screeches, in her best Bela Lugosi impression, "I vahnt my less-biansss!")

As a matter of fact, in 2004, Amy Lynn Best and I decided to try our own hand at "selling out" and set out to create our own exploitative lesbian vampire movie. (Amy's directive to me, borne from a frustrating film festival at which we witnessed very good movies passed by in favor of nudie fang romps, was "Write a movie about vampires in a brothel." The end result, *A Feast of Flesh* (changed from the original title, *Abattoir,* upon our distributor's directive—ironically, we were distributed by Camp Motion Pictures, whose sister label, Seduction Cinema, was the very company responsible for unleashing the very lesbian parodies that had permeated the marketplace), hit some of the right notes. We had nudity, a couple of lesbian vampire couplings, a decent amount of gore. But our storyline accidentally elevated us out of the "sell out" category. Instead of a cynical lesbian vampire cash-in, we wound up with a "vampire prostitutes

vs. the IRA", with no clear heroes or villains. We utterly failed in our goal to make a bucket of money off the bare backs of our vampire ladies. Too much story, not enough exploitation. It's a lesson we have, to this day, failed to learn. But as a connoisseur

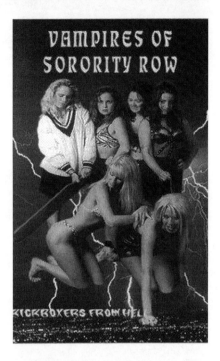

of low-budget entertainment, I'd like to offer some advice to any aspiring filmmakers who have somehow convinced their girlfriends to disrobe, don fangs and make out with their best friends in a new les-vamp opus. This may sound like nitpicking, but trust me, paying attention to certain details will go a long way towards raising your epic to a new level—even if you are only in it for the nipple shots.

**Rule #1: Vampires Don't Have Tan Lines.** Depending on which mythology you're going with, vampires either shun the sun or mildly dislike it. Generally, as portrayed in such non-lesbian vampire vehicles as

*Buffy the Vampire Slayer* (which has both lesbians and vampires, but not lesbian vampires, which is something they should amend soon if they want to continue to dominate in the ratings), vampires tend to explode upon contact with the old UV rays. Maybe all vampires are Irish, who

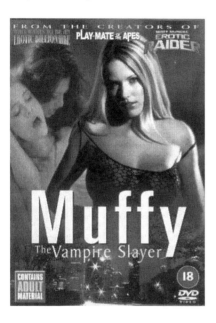

knows, but as a general rule, the bloodsuckers aren't morning, noon, or five o'clockish folk. And don't give me that bull about their having tan lines before they became undead. Just pat those white patches down with some body make-up. If your budget won't allow it, a can of flesh-colored Krylon goes for a buck a can at any hardware store. (I'm kidding. Do not spray-paint your actresses.)

**Rule #2: If the Fangs Leave the Mouth and End Up in the Cleavage, Chances Are The Suspension of Disbelief Will Go Right Out the Window.** I might still believe in the existence of lesbians, but you'll shake my faith in vampires every time.

**Rule #3: Even Lesbian Vampires Do More Than Writhe On Top of**

**Each Other**. I know you're just doing this for the sex, but for pete's sake, give these gals something to do once in a while. Have fun with it. What if your les-vamp is a perky, happy-go-lucky hippie type? Or a shy scullery maid who "seduces" more experienced members of the Sapphic Sisterhood? The world is your

oyster—and remember, oysters are aphrodisiacs. There are probably countless other rules, but you're making a lesbian vampire movie, so you're not aiming for high art here, right? Just do us all a favor. We appreciate the skin, but give us a little more "bite". (Did I just write that?)

Now, on the other hand, if you're going for lesbian werewolves...

Photo credits: P. 36 Sofiya Smirnova and Amy Lynn Best in *A Feast of Flesh.* Photo by Mike Haushalter. Top: Tina Krause and John P. Fedele in *The Vampire's Seduction. Bottom: Tina Krause. Same Movie. Copyright POPCinema. All Rights Reserved.*

**What Is Behind the Supernatural?**

By Dr. Rhonda Baughman

Mary and Carrie[2], two Jehovah Witnesses, wandered onto my porch early one Saturday morning clutching copies of *Awake!* magazine, (ironic, since I am *woke*, but not so much at 9am on a weekend), eagerly ready to discuss the topic on the cover: *What is Behind the Supernatural?*[3] Mary and Carrie seemed particularly convinced that Satan lives in the film industry (it's possible, I suppose)—but specifically within movies about witches, warlocks ... and vampires. This was a synchronous, meta moment for me.[4]

Not only had they interrupted my writing
progress on the short screenplay for *Expendable 2,* but these two sweet little ladies had no idea they were talking to a lesbian vampire of 14 years. How could they? I stood in direct sunlight, my front door boasted my reflection (looking very unawake and vaguely sex rumpled), I sipped coffee, not blood, silver adorned my ears and fingers, and many stakes peppered my property. So, of course they assumed I was human.

And I am—sometimes. Except when I become Rachelle Williams, who's been an onscreen lesbian vampire since 2003.

I love the screen and stage, actors and actresses, galavanting about in front of—and behind—the camera. I was born in the movies. Reborn, too. I'm slightly skeptical of death—I just imagine a screen wipe, then a new scene.

In 2003, for On Mark Productions' *Expendable,* I was Leslie—an obvious name choice for my lady-lovin'

---

[2] Original names did rhyme, but have been changed to reflect the author's dark humor: "Mary", as in American, and "Carrie" as in the King classic.

[3] Vol. 98, No. 2, 2017.

[4] I didn't have time to explain to Mary and Carrie why *Buffy: The Vampire Slayer* is the greatest TV series ever written nor why *Fright Night*, its sequel, *The Lost Boys,* and *Near Dark* remain classics beyond measure—as do so many more—so I simply nodded and thanked them for stopping by.

vampy sire persona opposite Ryli Morgan's nummy Nicole. The fangs were awkward, my outfits too tight, but the final scene holds the film's real Sapphic payoff—for audience and performers. No matter how silly some may view the film, it's found its fans—and really—those naysayers …did they have the privilege to act in a goddamn lesbian vampire film? I think not.

2007 hustled in and the shot rang out for me to frolic as another lesbian vampire—thistime as Carlotta, for Happy Cloud Pictures *A Feast of Flesh*. I preferred the working title of *Abattoir* but that was nixed early on for creative control purposes. I got to play tougher, conrol the handcuffs, punch my thumbs through a white hat's eyes, and roundhouse another good guy in the face—and all before letting loose with the mother of all screams. This role may have been therapeutic for me since, by then, I was a ten-year veteran of corporate-sadistically capitalist America.

I turned down a few more vamp roles to focus on writing projects, but in 2009 (through 2016), following the suggestion of Scream Queen Brinke Stevens, I joined up with Studio 588 for a series of quicksand vignettes, several shorts featuring, wouldn't you know … lesbian vampires. These shorts ranged from the comedic, to the deadly, to the sultry, before the

inevitable sink into the quicksand pit or the long, arduous struggle to free oneself from the pit entirely. Some scenes were solo, some duo, but all involved the gooey, sticky, vaguely heart-pounding sense of the sink. Some consider it erotic, but myself—like Brinke—found it a way to

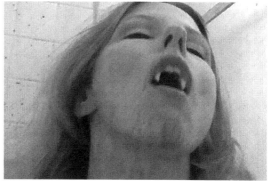

*Photo Credits – Top: Rachelle Williams and Alyssa Herron in **A Feast of Flesh**. Copyright Happy Cloud Pictures. Center: Williams as Leslie in **Expendable**. Bottom: Ryli Morgan as Nicole in **Expendable**. Copyright On Mark Productions. All Rights Reserved.*

cleanse/be reborn, renewed. Therapy I was paid for—so imagine that.

My roles in between these films and after, proved to be more or less human, with the occasional return to playing The Game of Flats: the closeted lesbian who makes out with a demon, and is subsequently slaughtered by another demon (Happy Cloud Pictures' 2009 *Demon Divas in the Lanes of Damnation*), a vicious lesbian demon favoring claw foot tubs and dragon kites (the unreleased Jess Franco/One Shot Productions' 2009 epic *Take-Away Spirit*), a dippy lipstick lesbian taught a valuable tongue lesson (Happy Cloud's 2008 release *Splatter Movie: The Director's Cut*), to just the asexual big sister who misundertands the younger lesbian sister (Henrique Couto's 2014 *Awkward Thanksgiving*), and finally to the we'll-let-you-guess-the-orientation zombie vamp cannibal mashup role as the Queen's Assistant (in Scott Barker's 2014 release *The Z*).

Once, twice, three times a straight, yet tarty, human for On Mark Productions: *Sin by Murder* (2004, released by Vista Street Entertainment), *Heaven Help Me, I'm in Love* (2005), and *Hardly Beloved* (2011). IMDB.com accurately lists a few other roles, but the latest—serving as Executive Producer for Full Moon Entertainment's 2017 *Evil Bong 666* proved to be an exciting new path for Rachelle. Yet, if called upon to return to my roots, I see no issue with that. Nudity never bothered me (and my, my, my, my Rachelle), nor do I believe in ageism. Not much bothers me really, except the hypocritically zealous and bombastic nature of many Americans' views on nudity and age. Oh, and whiney, self-entitled, passive-aggressive folks. And

Donald Trump. Shit—never mind. Quite a bit bothers me, come to think on it.

But being a real human off-screen, neither lesbian nor vampire, (rather pan and mortal) I'd like to think I did well all these years at playing. I've not had the opportunity to play straight vampire horror, but rather combinations of sexy, campy, dramatic, and fierce. And what began as amusement, a dare, and part of my curriculum, soon grew to represent a means of artistic homage and personal expression, and proof of a life lived well without restriction or fear.

I know JWs Mary and Carrie probably had good intentions, but we're too far apart in approach, interests, beliefs, and logic—and I don't have the patience to explain complex concepts to people who lack a contextual framework for my work, or that of my peers. And what I love is not up for debate—not with me, at any rate.

Besides, within my cobwebby trunk of dreams, I have lovely, fond recollections of all my time on film sets[5]—from my 2003 video debut to present and all of the unforgettable stops in between.

And I'm not done yet.

Hollywood might think all vamps need to be nubile and unblemished, but good artists know better, and great ones also understand they can do pretty much whatever they set their hearts and minds to. For both Rachelle and Dr. Rhonda Baughman, *that* is exactly what's behind the supernatural, as well as the formidable and the extraordinary.

---

5

imdb.com/name/nm1489995/?ref_=fn_al_nm_1

# A FASCINATION WITH NUDE VAMPIRES
# THE FILMS OF JEAN ROLLIN

By Mike Watt

French auteur Jean Rollin may be, and I don't say this lightly, the best-known of obscure horror directors, and the focus of his particular cinematic obsession was with our now-favorite topic, the Lesbian Vampire Film.

I will make the pretentious distinction here between "film" and "movie"—most of the narratives we review within these pages are "movies", aimed at entertaining the populace. "Films" are, at least to academics, something of "higher art", aimed above the heads of the unwashed masses who flock to "movies" to "be entertained". While Rollin aspired to capture the pocketbooks of French audiences desperate to escape the highly-charged political climate of the late '60s and early '70s, his style and focus belied his financial ambitions. The majority of Rollin's vampire work fall into that ephemeral category embraced by the French since the medieval era, namely *"the fantastique."*

As difficult to define for American audiences as the Spanish genre of "magic realism", *the fantastique* is a melding of horror, fantasy, science fiction, and the unexplained, with most of the emphasis on the latter. The primary distinction seems to be that while "magic realism" has fantasy and reality existing simultaneously with little to know barrier between, *the fantastique* moves seam-lessly between the two worlds as fantasy spills into reality and makes it unrecognizable, the narrative trapped in dream logic. Anything can happen, especially dark and dreadful things, without even an attempt at explanation. David Lynch works in a very shadowy corner of *the fantastique*. Jean Rollin seems to have been born there.

A cinephile at an early age, and the son of a stage actor who lived with his mother, Rollin became obsessed with the American serial during the 1950s, racing to the cinema after school to catch the latest episode of *The Shadow* (1940) and *Jungle Jim* (1948), which had been released to France for the first time since the end of the second World War.

"These were serials, always to be continued next week, so once an episode was over, nothing mattered but getting through the next week as quickly as possible!" Rollin told Peter

Blumenstock in 1995.[6] "The serials were not just a special piece of culture; they also had a real spirit to them, which changed our lives and attitudes. I certainly know, that these events are the source for most of the ideas that recur throughout my films. The spirit, structure and contents of the serial is the key to my type of cinema. I work from childhood memories, and even if I sometimes cannot name a film in particular, I know that all my ideas originated from that time."

While the American studios had become obsessed with the *noir* sensibilities of French cinema, the French were in turn eager to duplicate some of the lighter fare coming out of the U.S. Rollin was absorbing it all. Rollin further told Blumenstock, "When I was 15 years old, my mother gave me a typewriter, because she thought it might be useful if I knew

[6] *For **Video Watchdog #31**, published by Tim Lucas.*

*Above: Brigitte Lahie in **Rollin's 1979 Fascination.***

how to use one. That was an important moment; that's when everything started. I found a means of expressing myself. I began to write little screenplays and stories, heavily influenced by the films I saw. I adored Cecil B. DeMille's work, and when I was about 13 or 14, I became really obsessed with American serials. When I was a schoolboy, television didn't yet exist, so after school, I regularly went to the movies with my friends. The cinema and comic books were our whole lives! We were playing them, talking about them, living them."

Rollin "cut his teeth", so to speak, first as a teenager working for a firm that filmed industrial instructional videos, then as an editor in the French Army (in the '60s, young Frenchmen were required to complete a certain amount of military service). Fans of Rollin's may find this latter occupation a bit ironic as Rollin's films aren't known for their "montage" editing. Rather, the director prefers longer takes in his films, with a fluidly gliding camera either finding and revealing his subject or, more often than not, the subject entering the frame and the action unspooling in lingering, unbroken shots, sometimes more evocative of stage play than cinema.

But it's the action that unfolds before us that both entrances and repels. Fascinated by both the horror and eroticism of vampire lore, Rollin set the ante on sex and blood long before Hammer or the rest of Europe answered the call. For many, his films are frustratingly slow and borderline nonsensical. In the case of his first film, *Le Viol du Vampire* (*The Rape of the Vampire*), there's no "borderline" about it. Originally a short, 40-minute film largely self-financed, the injection of additional capital from American producer Sam Selsky, who would produce a number of his subsequent films, allowed him to shoot additional footage to bring the running time to feature length. The resulting black and white movie has a clear break in the film, with the new footage serving almost as a semi-sequel to the first half—indeed, some prints display a separate credit roll for both sections—with previously-dead characters revived and carrying on where their lives seemingly ended. (In attempting to sell the movie to theater-owners, Selsky, fully aware that the film made no sense, would talk constantly through screenings and immediately apologize afterward if the film seemed hard to follow due to his rambling. This occasionally worked.)

An experiment to be sure, the movie's theatrical run, almost completely self-financed by Rollin, was scuppered by political unrest lingering from the notorious May riots that tore through Paris in 1968. Since history is naturally compressed in hindsight, it was often erroneously reported that *Le Viol du Vampire* actually sparked the riots, despite opening later that summer. This is not to say that bewildered audiences, still on edge and in desperate need of escape, were unimpressed by the experimental storyline and presentation. Savaged by critics and audiences alike—one particularly enraged viewer called the film a crime and Rollin a criminal—Rollin almost gave up filmmaking entirely. However tempting it may be to attribute a political movement to an obscure vampire drama, in his article for *Senses of Cinema*, Simon Strong attempts to put this misconception to rest. "There are some obvious refutations to the courageous hypothesis that the riots of May 1968 were triggered by the premiere of Rollin's film: 1) most of the viewers of the film didn't riot, 2) most of the rioters hadn't seen the film, and 3) the film didn't open until after the riots had started," he wrote in April, 2004. Strong points towards one possible root of the legend: "[In the film] the Queen of the Vampires [played by Jacqueline Sieger] directs an amateur production within the film. The play presents a "blood wedding" of vampires. For no obvious reason, the audience (played by the Mob of the first part) revolt and trash the theatre. Consider then: the *stage* (of the blood wedding) is one frame of reference down from the audience in the *theatre* and, correspondingly, the *film* is one frame of reference down from the audience in the *cinema*. In the first instance, a riot breaks down the barrier between audience and actors. Meanwhile, in the higher frame of reference, the cinema audience are denied the possibility of disrupting the events in the film since it exists recorded in (eternal) cultural time. The psychic turmoil of audience demands an outlet that can only be vented through the disruption of the actual screening of the film."[7]

Thankfully, the allure of the silver screen was too great to ignore. In 1970, he released his second film, this one in color, *La Vampire Nue* (*The Nude Vampire*). By now, you're probably noticing a running theme.

Throughout his career, Rollin played with the tropes and conventions of Sapphic vampirism

[7] *Strong, Simon. 2004. "Sous la páve, le pláge!: Lesbian Vampires Vs the Situationist International." Senses of Cinema, Issue 31. April. http://sensesofcinema.com/2004/feature-articles/lesbian_ vampires_vs_situationist_ international/*

and crafted more than a dozen dreamlike loosely-structured narratives, casting his creatures as temptresses, fantasies, desires, and taboos, anything that would plague his "normal" protagonists who generally enter the films in the early stages of hetero-normative pairings. "Young lovers" are invariably corrupted, molested, abused, and/or destroyed by the lithe, oft-naked, fang-bearing creatures of his otherworldly, fog-shrouded night-scapes. His nubile blood-drinkers emerge from misty graveyards and foreboding forests, they inhabit moldering castles and posh apartments. They caress, they rejoice; sometimes they succumb, other times they prevail. Rarely do their actions resemble anything recognizable as mundane humanity.

Once he moved into color photography, his use of color, particularly reds and blues, became a motif of sorts, though he has insisted that this is unintentional, claiming he paid far more attention to the way things were lit and framed rather than how they were colored. More intentional were the political themes that found their way into his movies via metaphor. The elites eating the proletariat being a primary theme, as well as the male terror of emerging female power (political and economic as well as sexual) translated as bold sexuality. However, due to the surreal nature of his stories, almost any theme, real or imagined, can be superimposed over his films to suit every viewer's biases and suspicions. Arguments have been made that his films are fascist in nature; others insist they have a libertarian view. One sees in Rollin what one wants to see, and he seemed to be unable to care less about how others viewed his work.

Throughout the '70s, the Sapphic vampire remained foremost on Rollin's mind. Following *La Vampire Nue*, he directed *Le Frisson des Vampires* (*The Shiver of the Vampires*, 1971—see review), *Requiem pour un Vampire* (*Requiem for a Vampire*, also 1971), *Lèvres de sang* (*Lips of Blood*, 1975), and—after a break from vampires to create the moody zombie drama, *Les raisins de la mort* (*The Grapes of Death*, 1978, his most famous film on this side of the Atlantic), —in 1979, perhaps one of his most accessible, and argu-ably most beautiful and frightening (thanks to a marvelously evil per-formance from former pornographic actress, Bridget Lahie), *Fascination*. 1982 saw a brief return, resulting in *La Morte Vivante* (released internation-ally as *The Living Dead Girl*). All of which are rife with surreal imagery and strange eroticism.

As to why he found the vampire so fascinating, Rollin is frustratingly self-effacing. "That's difficult to answer. I don't really know," he told Blumenstock. "Maybe, because the vampire can be attractive, and certainly also because it gave me the possibility to show some nice girls not wearing very much [*Laughs*]! An erotic werewolf or an erotic mummy... I don't think so. Maybe it's also got something to do with my nature and the nature of my films. A vampire is like an animal, a predator-- wild, emotional, naive, primitive, sensual, not too concerned with logic, driven by emotions, but also very aesthetic and beautiful, and these are terms also often used when my films are being described. At least when they are being described by my admirers [*Laughs*]! [...] Honestly, I don't care

44

*Alexandra Pic as Louise, Isabelle Teboul as Henriette in Rollin's 1997*
**Les deux orphelines vampires (The Two Orphan Vampires).**
*Photo copyright Les Films ABC. All Rights Reserved*

[if I've been pigeonholed as a "vampire director"]. Some people say I'm a genius, others consider me the greatest moron who ever stepped behind a camera. I have heard so many things said about me and my films, but these are just opinions. I am perfectly happy with what I do, because it has always been my choice."

From the very beginning, Rollin's career was plagued by false starts, canceled projects, and ridiculous misfortune. A major distribution deal for his 1997 film *Les deux orphelines vampires* (*Two Orphan Vampires*, his first in over four years) was sabotaged by a smash-and-grab—thieves broke into his car and stole the first two reels of his work print, forcing him to re-edit from scratch and delaying the film's release. Work accidents, low budgets, and a lack of interest from

investors—all factors in Rollin's side-ventures as an academic (his essay on Gaston Leroux for the magazine *Midi-Minuit Fantastique* is considered definitive), a novelist, a comic book writer, and, when film work was especially scarce, a legitimate porno-grapher (1975's *Phantasmes* (aka *Once Upon a Virgin*) was his first and is notable for the only pornographic film in his filmography credited under his own name, due mainly to his own personal satisfaction in the resulting work). Uninterested in commercial fads or cinematic criticism, Rollin basically did what he wanted, damned the con-sequences, and moved forward. Towards the end of his career, Rollin suffered from both kidney failure and cancer. In 2007, he released what he'd intended to be his final film, *La nuit des horloges* (*Night of the Clocks* or *Night Clocks*). Meant

45

to be a "thank you/love letter" to his lifelong fans and supporters, the movie had elements of phantasmagoria, but had little spirit driving it forward. In 2009, his *Le masque de la Méduse* (*The Mask of Medusa*), this one more driven by Greek mythology, premiered on November 19, 2009 at the 11th edition of the Extreme Cinema Film Festival at the Cinémathèque de Toulouse, as part of "An Evening with Jean Rollin." Never released theatrically, the movie was distributed as a bonus with the first 150 copies of Rollin's book *Jean Rollin: Écrits complets Volume 1.* Dutiful pirates have since ensured the film could be seen by more than 150 people. Just a year later, Rollin was gone.

Both renowned and abhorred in turn by scholars of French cinema, Jean Rollin was the eternal outsider. Influenced by and a contemporary of the *Nouvelle Vague* ("The French New Wave" headed up by such luminaries as Alain Renais, Francois Truffault, and Jean-Luc Goddard), he was never considered part of the revolutionary movement. While the video label Redemption Video (whose own provocative—and R-Rated—production card sequence involves a vampiric fallen angel feasting upon the nude flesh of an initiate) has done its best to keep his catalogue in print, he still remains an obscurity in the United States, where so often gorehounds want their blood red, their women naked, their soundtracks dubbed, and their narratives linear, unencumbered by political metaphor and psychosexual conundrum. It's admittedly difficult to be ambivalent about Rollin—he's truly a love 'im or hate 'im kind of director. When he passed in 2010, he was mourned by thousands of horror fans. For the mainstream, his life was summed up in this obituary by Canadian press:

*"French horror moviemaker Jean Rollin has died. He was 72. The master of European B-movie thrillers died last week in Paris, France following a battle with cancer. He started his directing career in the 1970s and helmed a series of low-budget erotic vampire films, provoking outrage in conservative France with his sleaze-led horror projects. He went on to attract a cult following in the U.S. with B-movies including* **Requiem for a Vampire, Grapes of Death** *and* **The Living Dead Girl**. *Rollin is survived by his wife Simone, a son and a granddaughter."*[8]

Of course, for fans of his work, like his nubile living dead, Rollin will never die. For those eternally devoted to him, you can buy a special bobble-head statue of Rollin from CultCollectibles.com

*Above: Rollin.*
*Photographer unknown.*

---

[8] *"French horror director Rollin dead". Vancouver.24hrs.ca. 20 December 2010.*

Conducted by Doug Waltz

William Hellfire started his career when working with Michael Raso at the fledgling Alternative Cinema. Frankly, he became appalled at what people would buy from them. The no-budget softcore world did nothing for him and then Raso challenged him to do something of his own. His first film would be a sequel to Frank Terranova 1996 lesbian vampire opus, *Caress of the Vampire*, and in it there are the seeds of what would become his film movement, Factory 2000.

Using consumer grade VHS camcorders, he and his group of friends released a flood of bizarre, fetishistic films in a short period of time. His infamy was earned with the release of *Duck! The Carbine High Massacre*. Made a few short months after the Columbine School Massacre, the film was part condemnation, part satire of the tragedy, and shot in and around an elementary school in Ringwood, N.J., *Duck!* resulted in Hellfre and co-creator Joey Smack being arrested for possessing weapons on school property. Ironically, their legal fees were paid by sales of the movie. But this film was an exception to the Factory 2000's blinding focus on the fetish of strangulation and, sometimes, feet.

Hellfire continues working on behind the scenes documentaries for various video releases as well as making music with his band, Tyrannosaurus Dracula. Now, a true independent, Bill continues to make movies with his recent release of an exorcism going horribly wrong in *Upsidedown Cross* with Erin Russ.

This interview focuses on Hellfire's first feature and the genesis of *Caress of the Vampire 2*.

- Little known facts re: *Caress 2*:
- The first title of the film was *Caress of the Vampire 2 Teenage Foot Ghoul a Go-Go*. That VHS only existed as the first 50 or so copies. Title was changed and foot fetish toned down for the wide release.
- The band, "The Creeping Pumpkins," who appear on the sound track had Rick Sullivan on vocals Rick was the creator of the

47

underground fanzine gore gazette!

- Billy the Vampire appeared again in my second film, *Nude Strangle*, as a horror host introducing the film.
- Ruby Honeycat only made three films, *Caress* and *Nude Strangle* with me and *Guilty Pleasures* with Joe Zazo and Joe Parda. Ruby made the cover of *Draculina* magazine after the release of *Caress of the Vampire*.

**Exploitation Nation**: Since the film is *Caress of the Vampire 2*, why did it have nothing to do with the first one?

**William Hellfire:** The first *Caress* was a completely superficial soft-core vampire film. Basically an uninspired commercial venture with an unattractive cast, boring dialogue, and awful music. I didn't want my film to be associated other than by name.

**EN:** There's a scene with the one young man with the big grin and a girl who is stripping that I could swear was in another one of your movies. Was that scene from another film? It looks like it was in the basement.

**WH:** I think the uncut version of that scene was used in *Vampire Strangler*. That was Michi and Freak Nasty. Michi was also in *I Was A Teenage Strangler*.

**EN:** whose room of Christmas stuff is that? It is magnificent.

**WH:** That was my parents' house and my mother had horded all kinds of flower arrangement materials. She was a crafter and had given it up but never got rid of the materials she had acquired so we called it the 'flower room'. I loved in the basement apartment and shot most of my films there in the early days.

**EN:** You said this was your first film, what led you to making this film?

**WH:** *Caress 2* is my first film. Released Halloween, 1996, to an unsuspecting audience at Chiller Theatre. I was a telemarketer, part time, and I had just lost my job. I had provided two songs to Pete Jacelone for his first feature for W.A.V.E. Productions, *Psycho Sisters*. Pete told me that Mike [Raso, president of distributor E.I. Entertainment and its then imprint for erotica, Seduction Cinema] was looking for a salesman to help distribute VHS horror films. Mike and I both loved horror films so we got along pretty well. I was telemarketing from his office, selling SOV horror films to video stores. I started to watch some of the films I was marketing, like *Goblin, Sand Man, W.A.V.E.'s Most Gruesome Deaths*...and I was like...man these films are awful! So Mike told me to go make my own film. He lent me his S-VHS camera and gave me permission to make *Caress of the Vampire 2*. I added *Teenage Girl Ghoul a Go-Go*.

**EN:** The foot fetish aspect was that there to play to more than one specific audience to increase sales of the film?

**WH:** Actually the foot fetish was sort of a joke that was inspired by one Alternative Cinema [formerly E.I. Entertainment] customer who used to call the AC line looking for films with girls in white socks. Based on his request I added foot fetish to the plot. I knew I would have at least one sale!

**EN:** In a movie this weird I know weird stuff must have happened on a regular basis. What was the weirdest thing that happened?

**WH:** My friend and I were all from a punk rock background, we ran a cassette based recording label. We dropped acid together, played in each other's bands, put on rock shows in basements and legion halls so we were pretty used to the weirdness we created. I don't really remember anything too strange happening on the set. The soundtrack was mostly improved; most of the songs were recorded on the spot with only minutes of pre planning. What was weird really came after the release. After selling it at Chiller, Mike decided if we shot a new beginning on a high end broadcast camera we could probably get it into tower video. So I shot an extra night with the opening that appears on the most widely distributed version and sure enough it ended up on the new release wall at tower! The budget was less than $250 bucks total and here it was on the wall at Tower.

I totally forgot to mention, the *weirdest* thing about *Caress of the Vampire* was in 2002 A fan of the film got in touch with me with an idea to make a sequel to my sequel. He and his friends were big fans of *Caress 2* and they had already written a script. At first I had no interest in reviving the Billy the Vampire character and his humor was a bit different than mine, but as fate had it, I got a job working for Pete Jacelone in L.A. on *Das House* so I piggy-backed that into shooting a short strangulation/lesbian film *Strangled in L.A.* (about 40 minutes) long. Still unreleased but will come out soon on the *Lost Hellfire Tapes Vol. 2*) and *Caress of the Vampire 4: Fear of a Limp Planet* with Eric Eichelberger. Eric Directed the film and I just helped out with the structure of the production as well as acting in the film. Count Smokula was also in the film. I think we shot for 4 days, various locations and little sets being put together in people's apartments and houses. In this one Billy the Vampire is a pornographer and an evil anti-porn advocate gives bill and his crew weird meds that make them loose interest in sex and just want to knit sweaters. Eric made a DVDR release of it but shortly after that Mike Raso purchased the film and it was shelved. Supposedly Mike is doing a *Cares of the Vampire* box set so eventually it wills see the light of day. I still have my DVDR, the artwork is pretty cool.

**EN:** How did you achieve the cool dissolves throughout the film? Was that an in camera effect?

**WH:** The 'cool dissolves' were from a video toaster. We used just about every ridiculous one in the machine. Mike Raso was the editor on that film; he really gave it a 60's TV show vibe.

**EN:** What are Ruby and Michi up to nowadays?

**WH**: Ruby Honeycat and I split up in 1997. I think she works as a rep for a cosmetics company. Michi had substance abuse problems and died.

To learn more about our esteemed colleague, visit williamhellfire.com.

# THE KARNSTEIN TRILOGY
## HAMMER DOES SAPPHIC VAMPIRISM

By Mike Watt

If we're going to maintain our open and honest relationship here, I have to confess that I'm more a Hammer aficionado than an outright fan. Even during their heyday in the mid- to late-'60s, their budgets were minimal and it showed all over the screen. My favorite of their dubious trademarks included towns located on some strange time-split where it was often and simultaneously daylight on one side and misty night on the other. But where they lacked in money their movies made up for in atmosphere and a sense of otherworldliness. More importantly, they employed a pair of actors who lent gravitas to the proceedings: Peter Cushing and / or Christopher Lee. As long as one or the other appeared in the film, you were guaranteed some level of enjoyment.

For me, Hammer movies seemed to follow a standard beat sheet: Intriguing opening, usually bloody; then came the long middle part where carbon-copy young lovers, usually star-crossed, are introduced, their family feuds established, and perhaps hidden amongst all of this you'll get a fun set-piece involving fangs or monsters but always cleavage. Finally, an exciting climax and a bloody ending. Since Hammer was competing with larger production outfits they continually pushed their "blood 'n boobs" formula as hard as they could against the membrane of censorship also known as the British Board of Film Classification. Long before the board caved to pressure from self-appointed Minister of Decency, Mary Whitehouse, the BBFC during the Hammer years were actually pretty progressive, as far as censoring outfits go. This is largely due to the presence of Secretary of the Board, John Trevelyan, who considered the board as men who are "paid to have dirty minds." From 1958–1971, Trevelyan attempted to work with filmmakers and explain what cuts had to be made prior to a film's release.

Of course, that's his point of view.

Some filmmakers, naturally, felt that he was the ultimate enemy. Roy Ward Baker, who directed *The Vampire Lovers* and *Scars of Dracula* for Hammer, notoriously called Trevelyan a "sinister mean hypocrite", who played favorites with those he felt were in the "art house crowd" as opposed to commercial film directors. According to Baker and echoed by others, Trevelyan "kissed ass" with the bigger names in British Cinema. This relationship was sorely tested by Ken Russell and his still-controversial masterpiece, *The Devils*. While the two men warred over a sequence dubbed "the Rape of Christ" (a ten-minute scene that has only recently been restored to prints of the movie), John Hough took advantage of the distraction as he readied *Twins of Evil* for screens.

*Twins of Evil* is the third film of the so-called "Karnstein Trilogy"— the previous being *The Vampire Lovers* with Ingrid Pitt and its follow up *Lust for a Vampire*—all based on J. Sheridan LeFanu's ode to the Sapphic vampiric, *Carmilla*. Adapted by future rabble-rouser and trade unionist, Tudor Gates, the "Karnstein Trilogy" are perceived by some to be the last "great" films of the Hammer era, before their slide into utter poverty, and are notable for daring depictions of lesbianism, a theme that had gotten ten minutes chopped from "art house" film, *The Killing of Sister George*, in 1968, courtesy of the "progressive" Trevelyan.

As a trilogy, the "Karnstein" storyline doesn't really work, having no real continuity to speak of, except for the name of the evil family and their matron, Mircalla (aka Carmilla). The first film of the series, *The Vampire Lovers*, set film-goers all a-twitter with its boundary-leaping scenes of blood and nudity and girl-

vampire on girl-vampire action. The next two installments were toned down for British sensibilities.

*The Vampire Lovers* (1970), grew out of a perceived marketplace advantage. Hammer Studios, already competing for horror fans with other "upstart" companies like Amicus Productions, joined forces with Samuel Z. Arkoff and James H. Nicholson, and their company American International Pictures, best-known as the distributors of Roger Corman's highly-regarded "Poe" films (e.g., *Masque of the Red Death, Fall of the House of Usher*, etc.). The newly-permissive attitudes of the late '60s had allowed exploitation producers to push the boundaries of good taste, adding non-pornographic nudity to mainstream releases for the first time since Hollywood had self-proposed the Hays Code in 1930. Suddenly, breasts could be bared on the big screen, and Hammer was ready and willing to incorporate this immensely inexpensive form of production value for their films. With AIP, it was determined that Hammer would produce a new addition to its successful vampire series of films (begun with *Dracula* (aka *Horror of Dracula*) in 1958. This new film would adapt *Carmilla*. Not only did the Irish author Le Fanu's novel predate Stoker's more-famous *Dracula,* by 26 years, it explored female sexuality in a way that few other Victorian authors were brave enough to do. The narrator of *Carmilla* is the teenage Laura, whose family takes in Carmilla, the female ward of a mysterious countess, following a carriage accident. Laura and Carmilla share a psychic bond and, possibly, a mutual childhood dream. They grow inseparable, but Laura's father begins to fear for her health, which deteriorates as Carmilla grows stronger.

Eventually, after conferring with his friend General Spielsdorf, whose own niece recently withered and died under similar circumstances (involving a mysterious female visitor and an unhealthy relationship),

*Douglas Wilmer as Baron Joachim von Hartog, Peter Cushing as General von Spielsdorf and Ingrid Pitt as Marcilla/Carmilla/Mircalla Karnstein in* **The Vampire Lovers** *(Photo Copyright American International Pictures, Hammer Film Productions)*

Laura's father discovers that Carmilla may be the very same person as Mircalla, Countess Karnstein, a despotic aristocrat who'd died almost 200 years before. Joining forces with the General, and one Baron Vordenburg, descendant of a vampire-killing hero of the past, Laura's father pursues Carmilla to her native home to stop the evil from spreading further across Styria and the Austrian Empire.

*Carmilla* was adapted for the screen by Harry Fine, Tudor Gates, and Michael Style, with a screenplay by Gates which plays up the subtle horror and makes the relatively tame girl-girl attraction more explicit for modern audiences. In the book, Laura describes vivid dreams in which a giant cat bites her breasts. In *The Vampire Lovers*, the cat's face in Laura's dream becomes that of Carmilla's.

Multiple liberties were taken— Gates' script "tarted up" the story considerably, (according to *The Hammer* Story, written by Marcus Hearn and Alan Barnes), in order to make Le Fanu's episodic (the novel was originally serialized in the periodical *The Dark Blue*) more linear and cinematic, and some of these changes are as arbitrary and puzzling as those made in nearly every adaptation of Stoker's *Dracula*. For instance, *Carmilla*'s narrator, Laura, is now the doomed niece of General von Spielsdorf (Peter Cush-ing) and succumbs to "Marcilla" early in the film's first act, paving the way for Emma (formerly "Bertha" in the book) Morton, who pretty much serves the same purpose as Laura did in the book,

*Yutte Stensgaard as this go-round's Carmilla. (Photo copyright American International Pictures/MGM.)*

sensuality of the novel, albeit for sensationalism and titillation, rather than any attempt at exploring the Victorian mores and repressions that gave the book its throughline. As Carmilla/Marcilla, Ingrid Pitt is the embodiment of the "dangerous" female sexuality that caused English males such consternation.

While the movie may use Pitt's nudity, as well as that of Smith and Pippa Steel (who plays Laura) to its own cynical advantage, Pitt uses her undress as an example of her power, both as a means of seduction and control of her nubile victims. The same sexuality she employs to subvert the suspicions of the household's male butler is the same smoldering intensity she uses with the women. Carmilla is the ultimate sexual vampire, tricking her food into willing submission.

Strangely, AIP wasn't happy with the casting of Pitt, a relatively unknown Polish actress at the time whose only other role of note was in the ridiculously-entertaining *Where Eagles Dare* (1968) and an episode of *Doctor Who* from the swingin' Jon Pertwee (3rd Doctor) era. Their displeasure led to Hammer casting Cushing in a relative cameo as the General. AIP also pushed for sequel potential, leading Gates to write in a "man in black" character, played by John Forbes-Robertson (the only actor other than Christopher Lee to play Dracula, in *The Legend of the 7 Golden Vampires* (1974)), who appears only once on screen with any other character in the film and has little to do but sit in the background on horseback, laughing occasionally.

Of the relatively new ground of lesbianism and sex, producers Harry Fine and Michael Style, as well as director Baker, were more than a little concerned. "Po-faced," Pitt described

minus the narration or even any sense of substance. As played by newcomer Madeline Smith (who coincidentally also appeared in the notorious *The Killing of Sister George* and made her Hammer debut in 1969's *Taste the Blood of Dracula*), Emma is a pretty little bubble-head who easily falls prey to Carmilla.

More than its successors, *The Vampire Lovers*, captures the

53

them on the day of her first nude scene with Maddy Smith. On the other hand,screenwriter Gates when head-to-head with the BBFC's favorite censor, John Trevelyan. In a letter to Harry Fine, Trevelyan expressed deep concern about the script's content, saying that it contained "a lot of material that would we would be unhappy about even with an X at eighteen" (referring to an upcoming referendum in the House of Commons that would reduce the "X" certificate to 16 years of age requirement). For his part, Fine remained stoic, explaining that all of the objectionable material came from the source material—i.e. Le Fanu—and that they were simply trying to remain as faithful as possible to the book. Which tells you all you need to know about the machinations behind the war between art and "protecting" society.

Anticipating a hit, Hammer had already begun production on a sequel, *Lust for a Vampire*, then called "To Love a Vampire". Initially intended to be a direct sequel, Tudor Gates found his script rewritten by committee before the cameras rolled. Most of his callbacks to *The Vampire Lovers* would be excised. Much of the reworking was done so that production could be done at Bray Studios and nearby Oakley Court during a tight May-June schedule, in the hopes of getting a finished film to the screens by the end of the year. American backers AIP voted not to help finance the film, which hampered production immensely. To add to production woes, plans to shoot at Bray were scrapped in favor of the more-familiar Elstree Studios. Then, both prospective star Peter Cushing and director Terence Fisher were forced to drop out at the eleventh hour, replaced by Ralph Bates and Jimmy Sangster, respectively.

In *Lust for a Vampire*, Carmilla Karnstein, this time played by Danish actress Yutte Stensgaard, is again posing as aristocrat Mircalla, and enrolls in an all-female boarding school to satisfy her Sapphic urges as well as her need for phlebotomy.

*Above: Peter Cushing as Gustav Weil, having fun the Puritan way, by torching his niece, Maria (Mary Collinson) in **Twins of Evil**. (Photo Copyright Rank Organization.)*

Writer Richard Lestrange (Michael Johnson) becomes obsessed with the strange young girl and poses as a teacher to be near her. Meanwhile schoolmaster Barton (Ralph Bates, who later regretted his involvement in the film), covers up Mircalla's murders with a more insidious plot in mind. Forbes-Robertson reprises his role as "the man in black" and is actually given an identity this time around, as "Baron Karnstein". Not that he's given anything to do.

Feeling that he'd lost the battle over *The Vampire Lovers*, Trevelyan kept a closer watch over production of *Lust for a Vampire*. All of the lesbianism is downplayed now in favor of illicit hetero sex, despite the fact that Lestrange is, for all outward appearances, at least a decade older than Mircalla. A key scene between Mircalla and a nubile nudie schoolgirl named Amanda (played by Judy Matheson) was removed completely, while the central love scene between Stensgaard and Johnson was ruined in post-production by the intrusion of a terrible pop song—"Strange Love" by 'Tracy'. Reportedly, Sangster was "never so embarrassed" than when he witnessed the change at the film's premiere.

What could have been a fine successor to *The Vampire Lovers* was deemed a disappointment by the studio and pretty much all involved. Leaving aside the health issues faced by Cushing and Fisher, Hammer's greedy grab at another blood 'n boobs success left everyone unsatisfied. Had the proper time and money been spent, perhaps we'd have gotten a different *Lust for a Vampire*. But with installment three, Hammer seems to have learned its lesson.

While tamer than its predecessors, Hough's *Twins of Evil* exploits 1971's exploitative freedom by casting Playboy's first twin playmates, Mary and Madeleine Collinson, as the titular characters (no puns, please, we're British). Maria and Frieda Gellhorn arrive in Karnstein from Venice, two years after their parents died. They show up at their Aunt Katy's house in green, instead of the customary black-for-the-rest-of-your-lives. This enrages puritanical Uncle Gustav Weill (Cushing). "What kind of plumage is this? Birds of paradise?" But don't be too hard on Uncle Gustav, he and The Brotherhood have been busy burning witches all night, doing God's work. And by "witches", these Bible-wielding psychopaths mean

ONE USES HER BEAUTY FOR LOVE!
ONE USES HER LURE FOR BLOOD!
Which is the Virgin? Which is the Vampire ?

*TWINS OF EVIL*
"TWINS OF EVIL" starring PETER CUSHING
also starring DENNIS PRICE · MADELEINE & MARY COLLINSON · ISOBEL BLACK
KATHLEEN BYRON · DAMIEN THOMAS · DAVID WARBECK
Screenplay by TUDOR GATES  Produced by HARRY FINE and MICHAEL STYLE  Directed by JOHN HOUGH in COLOR
A HAMMER PRODUCTION
A UNIVERSAL RELEASE

"unmarried women", "women walking alone on a road", "old crones", anyone who has ever thought about having sex—you know, witches. In fact, the title sequence portrays one of these boys-being-boys bonfires after dragging a teenage girl forcibly from her home, lashing her cruxifix-style to a tree and then setting her on fire. And she screams and

*Hammer Heroines! Lying: Ingrid Pitt. Clockwise from left, Kate O'Mara, Kirsten Lindholm, Pippa Steele, Madeline Smith. Photo copyright American International Pictures / Hammer Film Production.*

screams as the "devils" flee from her "purified" body. In the back, Pat Buchannan nods approvingly.

Within seconds of arriving, the more-willful Frieda is ready to skip town as soon as she can find someone appropriately handsome and dangerous. One of Gustav's primary adversaries is Count Karnstein himself (played by Damian Thomas, best-known as the baboon prince Kassim in *Sinbad and the Eye of the Tiger*), a decadent lover, vague rulerand admitted Satanist who takes great delight in humiliating Gustav and his puritanical ways. Which, this early in the film, is a point in his favor since thus far Gustav has failed to win the hearts of the minds of the viewer.

But then we are whisked away to Castle Karnstein where the Count is being bored out of his mind during an actual Satanic pageant. Once he angrily dismisses the players, he finishes the sacred "stab the naked girl" ritual himself, evokes Satan but winds up with Mircalla instead. She makes him into a vampire (in a nifty shot in which she stands behind Karnstein but he alone is reflected in the mirror, and he watches himself fade away as he turns fangy). Before long, Karnstein is out to find something of Gustav's to corrupt and sets his sights on Frieda. Frieda is loved and admired by schoolmaster Anton (David Warbeck of Fulci's *The Beyond*)—literally, he can only see her, the rest is vaseline on the lens— when he really should be attracted to the more-demure Maria because... well, hell, she looks just like Frieda but she isn't a bitch. Besides, as everyone—everyone—points out, the two sisters simply cannot be told apart. Frieda exploits this by sneaking about at night and making Maria pretend to be her, so that Maria gets beaten twice (it's implied by not only Gustav but every patriarchal figure they've ever encountered). Strangely, Maria can sense when Frieda is hurt, but either Frieda can't feel Maria or just doesn't give a damn.

As typical of Hammer, no one heeds the vampire warnings (even though, apparently, there's already one running around long before the Count is turned during sex with his dead relative), more busty girls are either bitten or are flame-broiled by Gustav, and Frieda tramps around with Karnstein until she, too, is a mistress of the night. Her first task is to bite into the plump breast of Luan Peters (aka singer Karol Keyes) before the camera quickly cuts to anything else lest Trevelan wield his scissors.

If you've seen a Hammer film—any of them—you know what's going to happen. But Hough and Gates pull some nifty turns along the way. When Gustav catches niece Frieda feasting on one of the Brotherhood, he has her locked up so that he can make sure the rest of the family is safe, planning on burning her later. Sorry, purifying her later. But Karnstein manages to switch Maria for Frieda and soon it's the nice slutty twin that's heading to the stake and Hough plays this sequence to the hilt of suspense.

The second twist is far more subtle and involves Gustav's character, which more than proves Cushing's a master thespian. After he almost turns the incorrect niece into jerk chicken, Gustav's faith in his own crusade gets shattered. This is never discussed openly, but you can watch it work on Cushing's face. Used to the seat of power, when Anton presents Maria with a crucifix and she kisses—rather than sizzling beneath it like Frieda

did—Gustav is visibly shaken. While he never says it, it's clear he's wondering how many other innocent women have been put to death under

INGRID PITT · GEORGE COLE
KATE O'MARA and PETER CUSHING
, DAWN ADDAMS

ROY WARD BAKER
the HAMMER-AMERICAN INTERNATIONAL PRODUCTION
TECHNICOLOR

his pious wrath. We see a glimpse of his regret just as he's about to put the torch to Maria, refusing to pass it to his second in command—this isn't some random wench to be roasted for fun and, you know, "God's will"; this is his neice, who he swore to protect. The realization that he could very well have killed his own flesh and blood in the same manner as he had "purified" so many others chills him. After this sequence, Gustav still leads the Brotherhood but defers to Anton. "You're sure a stake to the heart will release [Frieda]? That her pure spirit will be saved?" For the first time in the film, we see all his noxious, prideful bull-puckey summed up in a question. Maybe the others in The Brotherhood were just out for a rollicking witch-burning, but Gustav honestly—honestly—believed he was saving the innocent souls of the wicked. Without the subtlety of

ONE USES
HER BEAUTY
FOR LOVE!
ONE USES
HER LURE
FOR BLOOD!

Which is
the Virgin?

Which
is the
Vampire
?

TWINS OF EVIL

"TWINS OF EVIL"
co-starring      also starring      starring PETER CUSHING
DENNIS PRICE MADELEINE & MARY COLLINSON ISOBEL BLACK
KATHLEEN BYRON DAMIEN THOMAS DAVID WARBECK
Screenplay by TUDOR GATES Produced by HARRY FINE and MICHAEL STYLE Directed by JOHN HOUGH in COLOR
A HAMMER PRODUCTION
A UNIVERSAL RELEASE

Cushing's performance revealing the man beneath the zealot, Gustav could have remained a villainous figure for the rest of the picture. While Count Karnstein is really the villain of the piece—with his fangs, his coiffure and cape—more than anything, he's just kind of a dick. He spends the climax in a vault, shoving out or dragging in one sister after another and locking the door again, taking few steps to take the upper hand. Gustav, for all his evangelical lunacy, was a man of action and principals. Yes, he shared Karnstein's arrogance, but he wasn't out burning witches every night because he was bored.

It's this last-act transformation that allows *Twins of Evil* to rise above its formula. It's not the first time Cushing has helped this elevation; each of his turns as Baron Frankenstein in the Hammer series shows a different man beneath the madness. But beyond the sex, blood, atmosphere and pretty photography, *Twins of Evil* gives the viewer something to think about, namely: think long and hard before you're convinced of your own righteous.

While much better than *Lust for a Vampire*, *Twins of Evil* suffered some indignities of its own that kept it from reaching a more properly respected status, this time not from the foes at home but moreso from Hammer's American distributor, CIC. After the MPAA's demands that all "exploitable" nudity was removed, as well as another 30+ cuts (equaling over five minutes gone) to violence and scenes requiring "pacing", CIC's Arthur Abeles wrote to producer Sir James Carreras, calling him "Jim Baby" and asking if the film could be retitled *Twins of Dracula* for the overseas release, in order to capitalize on that particular word so enamored by Americans. Carreras called Abeles' bluff and told him to feel free, provided CIC pay. Abeles agreed. And that's how *Twins of Dracula* hit the colonial shores, despite the fact that Dracula doesn't figure into the plot at all, singular or plural.

Ultimately, *Twins of Evil* marked the end of Hammer's most lurid period. While a fourth Karnstein film had been planned, alternately announced as *Vampire Virgins* and *Vampire Hunters*, was eventually cancelled. While a vampire member of the Karnstein family figures into the odd swashbuckler, *Captain Kronos: Vampire Hunter*, the Karnsteins as a family, and Carmilla as its most dangerous daughter, were finally laid to rest.

For the remainder of the '70s, Hammer Studios struggled against a withering economy and a dwindling interest in horror. Across the ocean in the U.S., the movie industry found itself dominated by the "Film School Generation"—Martin Scorsese, Francis Ford Copolla, Brian DePalma —who were creating grittier looks at the American Dream, while George Lucas and *Star Wars* gave audiences an insatiable appetite for special effects. As these and other films rippled their way through the world, the blood 'n boobs formula lost the race. A joint production with the Shaw Brothers, merging kung fu action with gothic adventure, *The Legend of the 7 Golden Vampires*, failed to gather any box office moss. An adaptation of Dennis Wheatley's novel *To the Devil a Daughter*, hoping to recapture the success they'd had with an earlier Wheatley story, the wonderful *The Devil Rides Out*, also failed to click with audiences. In 1979, Hammer released a remake of Hitchcock's *The Lady Vanishes* to lukewarm reviews and pitiful returns. By the time the calendar turned over to 1980, Hammer Studios was finished. It would be revived in 2007, but the dynasty was over, a stake driven through its heart by the very audience it has successfully seduced for two decades. The irony, it should be assumed, could not have been lost on the house that horror built.

Below: Bonus photo of Ingrid Pitt at **Countess Dracula.** Copyright Hammer Film Productions

# FRANCOPHOBIA

By Mike Watt

No discussion of lesbian vampires could ever be complete without an examination of the oeuvre of Jess Franco.

…So I guess this discussion is going to be incomplete.

# REVIEWS

Bill Adcock (BA), Matt Gilligan (MG) Mike Haushalter (MH), Douglas Waltz (DW), Mike Watt (MW)

**Blood and Roses (aka Et mourir de Plaisir, 1960).** D. Roger Vadim. The very first adaptation of Sheridan Le Fanu's *Carmilla* was as a segment of Carl Dreyer's *Vampyr* in 1932, albeit with all the lesbian allusions removed. In the second adaptation, Vadim keeps the same-sex attraction and jettisons the plot. And the characters. And anything else of interest.

*Blood and Roses* (retitled "And Die of Pleasure" to capitalize on his previous success, *...And God Created Women*) sets the story in the modern era of the late '50s and tells the story of a jealous Carmilla (Vadim's then-wife Annette Vadim) sulking about the engagement of her friend Georgina (empty-eyed Elsa Martinelli). During a costume party thrown by the groom, (Mel Ferrer, replacing Christopher Lee, as Leopoldo De Karnstein), a fireworks display unearths an ancient tomb. Investigating, Carmilla returns the next morning with a blood lust that can only be satisfied by female flesh. Or something like that.

While highly-regarded by fans of French cinema, as well as vampire aficionados, so much of *Blood and*

*Roses* lies inert on your screen. Gorgeous photography from Claude Renoir (nephew of filmmaker Jean Renoir, and who'd work again with Vadim on *Barbarella* in 1968) turns simple shots into works of art (Carmilla descending into the tomb as light arcs past a mist-shrouded chapel is the oft-published signature of the film), but the plot is nearly non-existent and the characters are all trapped in some Gallic malaise that limits their physical actions not unlike Michael Phelps attempting to swim through molasses.

The film's long history with censorship is another drawback to satisfying viewing. There are at least three different versions of the film floating around, none of which reflect the film's original running time of 87 minutes. The "official" French DVD restores a number of subplots, mostly concerning the vampire-obsessed preteen nieces, Martha and Marie, who spend most of the film spying on Carmilla's comings and goings. Yet, to fit in these kiddie hijinks, the film jettisons 99% of the film's most visual

*Elsa Martinelli and Mel Ferrer in **Blood and Roses**. Photo Copyright Films EGE Documento Film. All Rights Reserved.*

61

set piece, an elaborate dream sequence Carmilla seemingly forces upon a sleeping Georgina.

Carmilla leans close to Georgina and the film fades to an odd blue-black-and-white tint. Georgina "awakes" to see blood flowing from Carmilla's throat, beneath her necklace. Georgina is then led through a series of corridors, populated by strange-yet-familiar figures, until she finally reaches an operating room. Women in white robes and scarlet rubber gloves prepare a nude Carmilla for an operation. As the chief surgeon begins her first cut, she lowers her mask to reveal to Georgina that she, too, is Carmilla, that Carmilla is dead and is coming for the young bride.

Only the last shot, of Carmilla removing her mask and speaking of her own death, is present in the French version, and the editing is so abrupt—smash cutting from Georgina sleeping to the operating room—no longer in black and white but complete in oversaturated red—that making any sense of the shots is impossible without prior knowledge.

While the U.S. cut excises the children, it keeps the dream sequence more or less intact, including the brief topless scene, which must have been very surprising at the time. Both visually and thematically, this scene is the highlight of the film.

Ferrer provides the film its few moments of joy—from his delightfully bizarre "bat creature" costume to an excitedly playful scene where he plays a delirious piano game with Georgina—the rest of the cast emulates the somnambulant Caesar from *Cabinet of Caligari*. The brief kisses the women exchange are as devoid of passion as the film itself.

As Erich Kuersten wrote in his *Acidemic* blog:

[acidemic.blogspot.com/ 2011/03/ blood-and-roses.html], "An easygoing member of Parisian cafe society, Vadim's films are notoriously inert, and it's clear why: he's just *too satisfied*. As I wrote in AJFM #5's Pimps: The Devil's Subjects: You can't create tension if you've never been tense." This is by far the best summation of Vadim's work that I can find. There's never any urgency in a Vadim film, nor any sense of passion or even concern. This happens, then this happens, and it's all ever so tiresome. His movies languish on a fainting couch, eager to greet gentlemen callers and break the tedium. But the break never comes.

Still, *Blood and Roses* remains consistently high on "Best Vampire Movie" lists, so who am I to complain? (MW)

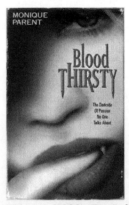

***Blood Thirsty (1999)*** D. Jeff Frey. *Blood Thirsty* is the tale of a young girl searching for acceptance and a place to live. When the petite rock star finds her way into the house of a nouveau vampire (all the bloodlust, none of the fangs or special powers), a bizarre relationship is formed. As the girl comes to accept the slashings and bloodletting in exchange for free rent, the vampiric seductress must decide whether it is safer for the relationship to continue or cut the new partner loose. This is a very anemic erotic thriller (and I use the term loosely). First off, don't let its appearance fool you, it is not a vampire film (or even a lesbian vampire film). It's a kinky fetish video about blood drinking—what's the difference, you ask?—well, vampires are usually rooted in the supernatural and this is a psycho-sexual addiction, in fact the whole story is like a three person play about control and addiction issues.

On the erotic side the film is very kinky in a dark side kind of way and the very beautiful Monique Parent shows off her flesh several times (as does the hunk Matt Bailey for you ladies). She also shares a torrid if tasteful lesbian scene with her co-star Leslie Danon. The only other cast highlight is Amazonian scream-queen favorite Julie Strain in a "blink and you'll miss it" cameo.

For the most part *Blood Thirsty* is slow-going and very talky enlivened only by a few scant sex scenes and a brief explosion of violence during the climax. About the only things it has going for it are its atmospheric lighting, Monique Parent's body, and a twist ending I didn't expect. Overall a strange viewing experience.

### *Caress of the Vampire* (1996) D.
Frank Terranova. A beautiful wo-man moves into her new home unaware that her neighbors are a pair of blood thirsty lesbian space vam-pires who want turn her into their undead lover! David F. Friedman use to say "sell the sizzle, not the steak" when talking about his work on exploitation films, and while I am taking his quote slightly out of context, I can say without hesitation that this lesbian vampire space stripper film is clearly missing the steak, and a good deal of the toppings on the baked potato. The film is 45-minutes of pure cereal fillers and flaccid stripper routines that feels much, much longer.

I will say that for what it's worth (and what it must've cost) *Caress of the Vampire* is a very movie-like effort put together by someone who was at least familiar with what a movie looked like and had a vague idea of how to tell a story even though they didn't have much of a story to tell. It's complete with all those things regular film goers expect such as establishing shots, fade edits, dialogue, location changes, and characters (such as they are). Another tid bit of interest is that the cast all seem to be adults and while none of them seem "old" they all seem much more mature than the casts that would populate the later films made by Seduction Cinema, *Caress'* main fault is that its *raison d'etre*—the "hot" lesbian couplings—are for the most part very poorly staged and underwhelming. The film's one woman-on-man scene is very clearly just a tepid stripper routine filmed in glorious real time. The final "climatic" seduction scene comes close to being erotic but it's too little too late and ends before it really gets started. I normally would try to praise this or that actress or actor for the good job they did or something at this point but no one has a name in the film so I don't know who to praise even if I had some praise to give, which, frankly, I don't. Really, the actresses were attractive and the men folk as the cops remembered their lines, so what more can you ask for? (MH)

### *Caress of the Vampire 3: Lust of the Night-stalker (a.k.a. Muffy the Vampire Slayer)* (1999). Written and Directed by Mario Cima-devilla. Starring Hannah Cole-man, Lucy Gresty and Louise Hodges. Kathy is

Caress of the VAMPIRE
...Lust is Timeless

an under-cover cop who is following up on the reports from the previous cop from *Caress of the Vampire 1*. It seems that a new alien lesbian vampire is in town killing girls left and right. Kathy goes on the trail and something stirs up inside of her. She acts on these feelings by hiring a female prostitute to have sex with. Her husband is tired of her police work and walks out on her.

Kathy has discovered that the alien lesbian vampire has little discretion in her victims so she takes a bath, then she takes a shower and then she reads some books before going on the hunt. She knows that her body will be the perfect trap for this monster. If the monster doesn't get her first.

*Caress of the Vampire 3* is an awful lot like the first entry in this series. There are a lot of ample women prancing in front of the camera showing off their goodies, usually in slow motion. This sequel is five minutes longer, but I think that might have something to do with a sex scene being recycled from the first one. The computer generated footage of the alien space ship are just the same ones created for the first film so, I do commend the film makers on their thriftiness. The dialogue is the same, badly dubbed nonsense from before and the scenes of girls rubbing on each other just seems to take forever. There is a much higher body count in the film even if it is mostly a bloodless affair. The one true saving grace is two curvy females wearing nothing but their birthday suits throwing down in a fight to the death with a huge wooden stake being waved around. Comes at the end of the movie though, so it's a bit of an endurance test to get there.

Maybe you can just fast forward to that part. It does make the film. While the production date of this movie was 1999 it never saw release until 2005, probably to capitalize on the whole *Buffy the Vampire Slayer* thing, which is odd when you consider that show went off the air in 2003.

Oh well, there are boobies. I did mention those, right? You were really only going to watch this for those anyway, right? Sure, there are the vampire's boobs which look like some plastic surgery experiment that went horribly wrong, but everyone else seems perfectly natural. Okay, maybe not natural, but not freakish. They are fake, but not really fake. I am glad that Seduction Cinema decided to end this little series with this one. I think the potential of an Alien Lesbian Vampire sounds great, but you need to make a movie out of it, not naked women grinding in front of the camera for 45 minutes. That's not a movie, that's a Grindhouse loop that is overstaying its welcome. (DW)

***Daughters of Darkness (1971).*** D. Harry Kümel. Newlyweds Stefan (John Karlen) and Valerie (Danielle Ouimet), on their honeymoon, in Belgium, check into a lavish hotel. Relishing the privacy granted by the off-season, Stefan and Valerie have

*John Karlen, Danielle Ouimet, Delphine Seyrig. Copyright Ciné Vog Films.*

the whole joint to themselves until the mysterious Hungarian countess, Elizabeth Báthory (Delphine Seyrig), arrives with her "secretary" Ilona (Andrea Rau). The hotel's matre'd remembers the Countess from a previous stay, 40 years ago, when he was but a boy. Before too long, the amiable and enigmatic Countess takes a shine to the young couple, and Stefan, in turn, begins to covet Ilona, taking his violent frustration at her disinterest out on poor Valerie. In the meantime, the Countess shares tales of her lonely life with the abused bride, slowly luring the girl towards a darkness she'd never known before. One of blood and eternal night time.

When it comes to lists of "classic" gothic vampire stories, *Daughters of Darkness* can usually found in a respectable position near the top. Legendary feminist author Camile Paglia, of all people, declared the film to be "classy" and an example of "high Gothic" drama. In her seminal 1990 book, *Sexual Personae: Art and Decadence from Nefertiti to Emily Dickinson*, Paglia wrote: "High gothic is abstract and ceremonious. Evil has become world-weary, hierarchical glamour. There is no bestiality. The theme is eroticized western power, the burden of history."

Unlike most films in this subgenre, *Daughters of Darkness* is a triumph of production design and atmosphere. Gorgeous photography courtesy of Eduard van der Enden shows off not only the scenery—particularly the opulent Hotel Astoria, in Brussells, which provided the film's interiors, and the lush Royal Galleries of Ostend.

The actors are equally lovely, from the unlikable Karlen, to the bland-but-beautiful Ouimet, who is the object of the plot, rather than an active participant. Veteran actress and European movie star Seyrig is decked out in reds, whites, and blacks, reportedly to evoke Marlene Dietrich's Nazi-chic from *The Blue Angel*. Andrea Rau, the most-interesting and energetic of the quartet, sports a Louise Brooks bowl-and-bangs cut, giving her a look that's unique to the film's predominant blondes, at the same time reminding one of Italian artist Guido Crepax's oversexed heroine "Valentina" (a look replicated in 1973's adaptation *Baba Yaga*, the character played by Isabelle De Funès).

Yet with all the visual beauty, the story is spare—a subplot involving young girls found murdered across the country is barely addressed—the pacing glacial, and the eroticism lacking in nearly all respects. Stefan and Valerie's con-summation is washed in blue but absent of any kind of passion. The one instance where

Seyrig and Ouimet are meant to share a kiss, the camera lingers on their lips but cuts immediately away before they touch. The next shot is of the back of Ouimet's head, as Seyrig moves her own face around in the background, very obviously nowhere near Ouimet's face. This "that's as close as you're gonna get!" sequence is repeated when Seyrig is meant to be feasting upon the blood of a victim. A trickle of red is seen, but her mouth is miming at a different geographical part of the body.

For fans of European art films, *Daughters of Darkness* offers a visual treat, but you get the same from anything by Jean Rollin—just as gorgeous, but at least twice as lurid. And at least when Rollin's stories don't make sense, there's usually enough going on to distract you from the confusion. (MW)

**The Erotic Rites of Countess Dracula (2001)** D. Donald F. Glut. Way back in the sixties sexy Scarlet Brooks' "big break" as a rock star is cut short by Count Dracula! The next night, Scarlet rises from a coffin in Dracula's castle as one of the immortal undead, guarded by the Count's crazed, bug-eating servant Renfield. Scarlet despises her new existence as a vampire, and after savagely satisfying her craving for blood by victimizing a friend, she accepts her fate but vows never to attack another human being again.

35 years later, Scarlet (now known as the "Scarlet Countess"), jaded and depressed, survives on outdated blood acquired from hospitals and blood banks. Tired of her life as a vampire she orders Renfield to drive a stake through her heart. Unable to destroy Scarlet, Renfield discovers that if a vampire can get three virgins to sacrifice their blood willingly in a single night, she can become mortal again. Embarking on this seemingly impossible quest, Scarlet stalks and seduces three young beauties, making passionate love to each one and finally feasting on their blood. But, as they say, "be careful what you wish for."

I really liked this super-sexy erotic vampire film from Seduction Cinema and Frontline films. Originally named *Scarlet Countess* the film was given the more exotic and marketable title *The Erotic Rites of Countess Dracula* for DVD/Video release. Writer-director Donald F. Glut puts together a very satisfying low budget lesbian vampire film here. His previous work includes *Dinosaur Valley Girls* (which he wrote and directed as well), scripts for *Land of the Lost* and *The Scooby Doo and Dynomutt Hour*, as well as some horror novels based on the classic monsters. Shot in only five days, Glut's love for vampire lore, filmmaking and beautiful woman shows on the screen and in the playful script. Extra kudos, too, for a script that is rather good and has an actual story, which is a rare thing for a nudie-cutie film. The film looks very good for being shot on video. It has tight editing; well-constructed shots with lots of fluid camera movement, and the several lesbian couplings are all well staged and filmed. Even the scenes set in the sixties are fairly well presented, which is no mean feat considering video just screams nineties. The best scene is Scarlet's dream sequence that has a nice old news footage effect. The cast is great, featuring an awesome cameo by William Smith (*Any Which Way You Can*), as Dracula. Smith's portrayal of Dracula adds a lot of credibility to the film and boosts the performances of cast members playing opposite of him. Renfield, played by Del Howison (who in real life owns the bookstore that was used for location shots), does a good job as Scarlet's right hand man. More importantly for a film of this type the starlets are all hot, sexy and decent actresses. Brick Randall is very good as the star vamp Scarlet and is very sexy, voluptuous, and handles the role of lead with ease and poise. Goth Girl store clerk, Shado, played by Julia Anna Thurman, is the film's crown jewel however, a pale thin exotic beauty with coal black hair and small pert breasts with large perky nipples. Her erotic encounter with Scarlet is the high point of the film and is worth the price of purchase alone. Her facial reactions of bliss are some of the most erotic I have ever seen. She's easily the hottest girl in this film. The Goth inspired soundtrack is also good with a few tracks I wouldn't mind having on CD. All in all this adds up to one fine flick. I'm looking forward to seeing the proposed sequel *Crimson Tears* but for the meantime I think I'll go rent *Dinosaur Valley Girls* for a future review. The Seduction Cinema DVD contains several nice extras including an excellent audio commentary with director Donald F. Glut and crew, a blooper and outtake reel, and a whole heap of cool previews are also featured. (MH)

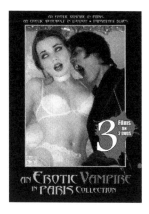

*An Erotic Vampire in Paris* (2002) D. Donald Farmer. Caroline, an innocent young American tourist (Misty Mundae) depressed by the recent death of her mother meets beau-tiful Parisian vam-pire Isabelle (Tina Krause), and begin a passionate lesbian affair. But when the relationship is threatened, will the girl's lover give in to her insatiable thirst for blood?

*Erotic Vampire in Paris* is one of the hottest Seduction Cinema releases ever. It is a sexy, dreamlike lesbian vampire tale filled to the brim with lush visions of naked flesh courtesy of the very voluptuous Tina Krause, credited in this picture as Mia Copula, and Seduction Cinema's crown jewel, the Lolita-like Misty Mundae.

Plot-wise, *Erotic Vampire in Paris* is dialogue light, preferring to tell its story through lush dream like photography instead of scenes of long exposition. In a sense the film is rather reminiscent of the erotic Euro-classic *The Bare Breasted Countess*.

Tina Krause is the film's titular vampire, a role she plays to the hilt with languid sensuality, smoky eyes, and a European accent. Misty, in one of her better roles, is a displaced American tourist. As on screen lovers the two young ladies share great chemistry and their long lingering kisses seem very authentic. William Hellfire is also on hand as a voyeuristic victim.

*Erotic Vampire in Paris* was made in France by director Donald Farmer with beautiful cinematography courtesy of Merril Lucas and second unit work by William Hellfire. The change of locale to France from America and the foreign crew really gives this film a mature shine lacking from its competitors and sister films. In fact, the film looks much more like one of Jean Rollin's erotic horror classics than one of the countless American lesbian vampire efforts. (MH)

**Frisson des Vampires, Le (*The Shiver of the Vampires*, 1971).** D. Jean Rollin. Newlyweds Isle (Sandra

*Dominique emerges from a clock in*
**Frisson des Vampires.**
*Photo copyright Les Films ABC.*
*All Rights Reserved.*

Julien) and Antoine (Jean-Marie Durand) travel to a chateau to meet Isle's cousins, whom she hasn't seen since she was a child. Upon arriving

in town, they're informed that the cousins had died only the night before. At the cousins' chateau, the pair are greeted by two grim-faced maids (Marie-Pierre Castel, Kuelan Herce) who make up their room. At midnight, a woman emerges from the grandfather clock in Isle's room. She introduces herself as Isolde (model and actress Dominique) and proceeds to first seduce her and then drink her blood.

Meanwhile, the cousins (Jacques Robiolles, Michel Delahaye) reveal themselves to be still alive, albeit as foppish poofs in frilly clothing and grey faces. While insisting they are vampire hunters, it's pretty plain that they're members of the undead themselves and under Isolde's control. It'll be up to Antoine to rescue Isle from their nefarious plans, but Isle seems to be all for joining the ranks of the undead. Can the cousins break free of Isolde's powers—she's already impaled another woman via spiked metal pasties that pierce her victim's breasts!—or will they give their living cousin over to their vampire queen.

Rollin's third feature, *Le Frisson des Vampires*, is beautiful to watch and frustrating to pay attention to. Less dreamlike than *Le viol du vampire* (1968) or *La vampire nue* (1970), *Frisson* struggles to maintain a narrative consistency. If we take as writ that Isolde is controlling all the other inhabitants in the castle, then many of the film's oddly-shaped plot holes caused by inconsistent character motivation can be forgiven because they're not fully-realized as people. Isle is the object—desired by Isolde, claimed via marriage by Antoine,

68

something to either be exploited or protected by the cousins, but never a whole person in and of herself. Isle only exists as a reflection of those beholding her, audience included. This time around, Rollin's lack of funding leads to some marvelous verisimilitude, particularly with regards to the crumbling, rotting chateau where Isolde and the cousins reside. The chateau is as much a metaphor for the disintegrating aristocratic structure as it is a wondrous setting for the action. Other critics with whom Rollin clashed repeatedly over artistic differences. Newman found that *Frisson* "contains some of the most banal imagery in the Rollin catalog. Virtually all the scenes are brightly lit, destroying any potential for an eerie atmosphere. Even the much ballyhooed scene where a female vampire emerges from a grandfather clock is clumsy and ludicrous." Still, there are a lot of interesting things going on, both visually and thematically. Rollin's musings on religion and politics are given a lengthy platform in an alternating dialogue delivered by the cousins during a dinner scene, explaining how Christianity developed the personae of the Virgin Mary by inverting the sex of the pagan "Horned God" and modifying the Egyptian creation myth of Isis. This, the cousins argue, allowed early persecuted Christians could have it both ways—they could argue that the "Horned God" was not female nor Isis because God is one being in three; they could argue that the perceived idolatry was not blasphemous because the Horned God was an image of a woman and, therefore, "not God." It's an interesting argument, though it's placed ponderously in the middle of the film, just as we felt we were getting our bearings with the plot.

For what it's worth, it's the film's more contemporaneous touches that produce the most surrealism, particularly the incongruous, guitar-heavy rock score from band Acanthus, and the occasional "hippie" touches to the costume design. Both elements are completely out of place in a gothic horror film, but at the same time they seem *deliberately* out of place, additional elements to keep the viewer off-balance.

While Newman warns that viewers new to Rollin do not start with *Frisson,* I'd argue the opposite. It's actually not a bad place to start, as far as his catalogue goes. It contains all the elements he would explore in other films—vampirism, nudity, Sapphism, politics, polemics, sexual sophistication—and eases the unfamiliar into his style and sensibility.

On the other hand, as far as I'm concerned, one would do better to start with *Fascination* and work backwards, but to each their own.

***The Hunger (1983).*** D. Tony Scott. Vampire Miriam Blaylock (Catherine Deneuve) is hundreds of years old and lives in a beautiful New York townhouse with her relatively young (200 years young) lover, John (David Bowie). They haunt the NY club

*David Bowie, Catherine Deneuve, Susan Sarandon in **The Hunger.***
*Photo Copyright MGM/UA. All Rights Reserved.*

scene, trolling for new victims upon which to feed. Without warning, John begins to age exponentially over just a couple of days. Realizing that her promise of eternal life did not come with eternal youth, John seeks out a gerontologist, Dr. Sarah Roberts (Susan Sarandon), who, with Tom Haver (Cliff DeYoung), studies advanced aging in primates. John thinks her work might lead to a cure to his advanced decrepitude, but Sarah dismisses what she sees as an elderly man who may be in the throes of dementia. Desperate, John murders one of Miriam's students, drinking her blood but failing to reverse his aging. Arriving home, Miriam discovers two bodies to dispose of. She makes short work of "disappearing" Alice, but John is another matter. Through the centuries, all of Miriam's lovers have succumbed to this living death,

but she cannot bear to release them from misery. She places him inside a coffin in the attic, alongside dozens of other such coffins, leaving him to moan in despair with the rest of her trapped "family".

Feeling guilty about the way she'd treated John, Sarah goes to his address but finds Miriam instead. She's surprised at the almost instant attraction she feels towards Miriam. They drink wine and have sex, during which Miriam reveals her true nature. Sarah is both fascinated and repulsed at the "lifestyle" of drinking blood. Her budding relationship with the vampire leads to conflict with Tom, both professionally and personally (Sarah and Tom are in a supposedly committed relationship). Worse, they discover that some kind of infection is taking over the healthy cells in Sarah's bloodstream, contracted from ingesting Miriam's blood. Sarah is rapidly becoming a being like Miriam, with the need for blood clouding her judgement, making her hunger beyond reason. Which leads Sarah to a horrible question: what if you could live forever, but only as an addict? This question leads to even more horrible answers.

Hip and stylish almost at the expense of substance, *The Hunger* is a lesbian vampire film that has gained respect over the years. A loose adaptation of Whitley Streiber's (*Wolfen*) novel, *The Hunger* skirts over the questions its narrative raises, burying much of the moral plot beneath a veneer of beautiful photography, excellent composition, and a heart achingly beautiful soundtrack courtesy of Howard Blake (who makes marvelous use of Delibes' *Lakmé* performed on cello). Dismissed by contemporary critics— Roger Ebert called the film "agonizingly bad"—time has improved its cinematic standing, with Camile Paglia going so far to classify it as "classy" in her 1990 book, *Sexual Personae.*

Because of its *Rocky Horror Picture Show* connection—with Sarandon ro-mancing DeYoung, her "Brad Majors" counterpart in *Shock Treatment—The Hunger* is also a movie that tends to be rediscovered every few years by the obsessive *RHPS* crowd, mainly for the chance to witness Janet Weiss's relatively explicit lesbian coupling with Deneuve. It's also a hit among old school goths, thanks to an appearance by Peter Murphy singing the Bauhaus' hit "Bela Lugosi's Dead" during the opening sequence.

For fans of this particular sub-genre, *The Hunger* is one of the very few American-made movies that comes close to replicating the bizarre beauty of Jean Rollin. It also suffers from the same maddening narrative disinterest of Rollin's films. The story is fairly muddled, if not confusing at times, especially when parsing Sarah's motivations. The addiction question isn't raised until almost the end of the film, long after Bowie has departed. MGM enforced a tacked-on ending, showing that Sarah has seemingly replaced Miriam—despite also seemingly having committed suicide to destroy Miriam—in the hopes of producing a sequel should the box office warrant one (it didn't), the film's final moments undercut everything that came before it, leaving whatever message of "realistic vampirism" left over from Streiber's novel buried beneath the detritus of Scott's oppressive style. (On the DVD audio commentary Sarandon is particularly vocal about her disapproval of this forced dénouement.)

What we're left with are some wonderfully bloody moments, wondrous old age make-up courtesy of the late maestro, Dick Smith, and the central icon lesbian coupling between Sarandon and Deneuve. (I also must confess to a Mandala Effect with regards to different cuts of the film. My first viewing was a network TV broadcast which eliminated most of the lesbian scene, but added a sequence of Sarah graphically murdering Tom on-screen. I have never witnessed this scene again, leading me to wonder if I imagined it. Wouldn't be the first time as I *definitely* remember seeing *Shazam* with Sinbad, despite knowing intellectually that this film does not exist.) All in all and in the end, everyone is right. *The Hunger* is classy, yet messy, both an art-house film and a cynical commercial splatter. It aged better than any of Miriam's former lovers, but yet is trapped in the era in which it was made, very '80s, very New York, all of a previous time. Still and all, it was an expensive, mainstream Hollywood production about lesbian vampires made with major movie stars. Not for nothing, that alone makes it notable. (MW)

***Jesus Christ Vampire Hunter*** (2001; **Odessa Filmworks**) D. Lee Demarbre. The lesbian pop-ulation of Ottawa, Canada is being threatened. Daughters of Sappho disappearing nightly, turning up drained of blood if at all. Under-standably, this has the Catholic Church deeply concerned, and a mohawked, studded-vestments-wearing priest is dispatched on a moped to ask Jesus Christ (who has ap-parently been back for some time, and has just been relaxing on a beach somewhere turning water into lemon-ade) to intervene. One shave, haircut, and mixed martial arts fight with a clown car's worth of atheists later, Christ is ready to take the fight to the vampires who have been preying on Ottawa's lesbians. After getting his righteous ass handed to him by kung-fu nosferatu, Christ recruits Vatican gunslinger Mary Magnum and luchador El Santo to help him bring an end to the bloodsuckers' reign of terror.

This film is undeniably weird. The first feature-length production from Odessa Film-works, it has a definite "kitchen sink" vibe that many first-time independents do—the opportunity for a second movie might not come along, so why not go for broke with the first? *Jesus Christ Vampire Hunter* is certainly a little rough around the edges, but undeniably a labor of love, fueled by a love of genre films and a silly, somewhat subversive sense of humor. Not everyone would make a film about Jesus Christ killing vampires to protect lesbians, but here we are and the world is better for it.

And it is a film that should be lauded for its creativity—from the endless ways in which vampires are killed (including exhaling hard in one's face after the consumption of an extra-garlicky shawarma and 'staked' with a thrown drumstick) to the truly grotesque frat-boy mad scientist, director Lee Demarbre and screenwriter Ian Driscoll (who also plays lead vampire Johnny Golgotha) spared no opportunity to do something fun with the film.

While *Jesus Christ Vampire Hunter* is about as irreverent as they come, its warmth and affectionate presentation make it hard to claim blasphemy. We're treated to reenactments of the Parable of the Good Samaritan and the Sermon on the Mount, while Christ's stern admonishment that "there's nothing deviant about love" in defense of LGBT+ individuals in the film is a welcome one. Not everything in the film makes sense—the Rasputin-esque narrator jumping out of bushes comes to mind—but it's too much fun to care. Be prepared to hum the catchy

closing tune, "Everybody Gets Laid Tonight" for weeks. (BA)

***The Lair of the White Worm* (1988; Vestron Pictures)** D. Ken Russell. Bram Stoker is known primarily for *Dracula,* though this was hardly his sole foray into horror; *The Jewel of the Seven Stars* is a mummy story, while the short story "The Squaw" is a Poe-esque tale of revenge. *The Lair of the White Worm,* first published in 1911 and later revised and drastically shortened in 1925, is a story of ancient survivals and sinister femme fatales. It's also, ah…not good. The 1925 edition is almost unreadable given how severely it's been hacked up, and in either case it is more racist than H.P. Lovecraft scripting episodes of *Amos 'n Andy.*

With the novel falling fairly swiftly into the public domain, it would inevitably be made into a horror film; what is perhaps less inevitable is that Ken Russell would be the man to direct it. Russell at this point had already developed a reputation for eccentric projects and for combining religious and sexual imagery.

Russell's film follows archaeology grad student Angus Flint (a young and wild-haired Peter Capaldi), who discovers an enormous reptilian skull in a Roman ruin in Britain, on property owned by Mary and Eve Trent (Sammi Davis and Catherine Oxenberg, respectively). The skull is identified as connected to the local legend of the D'ampton Worm, a dragon-like creature; researching the legend brings Flint into contact with the current Lord D'ampton (a very young Hugh Grant). It also brings them into conflict with local eccentric Lady Sylvia Marsh (Amanda Donohoe), who, as a deathless, inhuman priestess of the D'ampton Worm, has designs for both the skull and Eve Trent.

Russell wisely jettisons the racism and boring shit of the novel, replacing it with every possible inclusion of serpent imagery (including an old copy of the board game Chutes & Ladders, when it used to be called *Snakes & Ladders*) and as much rampaging sexuality as possible; the idea of the snake as a symbol of the erect phallus is very much in play in this film, and Russell isn't afraid to go in the opposite direction, and give us an erect phallus—specifically, a wine bottle-sized, bladed strap-on dildo worn by Lady Sylvia late in the film—symbolizing a snake! While the D'ampton Worm—here an almost Lovecraftian god-monster—is an impressive monster, Lady Sylvia is the more immediate threat, with retractable fangs and an ability to spread her serpentine nature to her victims, a contagion owing more to the Stoker's Transylvanian count than to the White Worm. (BA)

***Lust for Dracula (2004)*** Written & directed by Tony Marsiglia (*Dr. Jekyll and Mistress Hyde*), *Lust for Dracula* is a sexy, stylish re-interpretation of the classic Bram Stoker story that weaves a dark and

tragic tale of madness, obsession, drug addiction, transformation and death. Mina Harker (Misty Mundae) isn't the happiest of Hollywood Hills wives— even though she's married to wealthy pharmaceuticals magnate Jonathan Harker (Julian Wells). The repressed Mina longs for Jonathan's love and the happiness a child would bring them, yet the arrival of the beautiful and mysterious Dracula (Darian Caine)— seductive vampire servants at her side—will change their lives forever. Dracula offers Mina the sensual existence she so desperately craves— one that is immediately threatened by Mina's sister, Dr. Abigail Van Helsing (Shelly Jones). Van Helsing seeks to not only destroy the monstrous vampire but also covet Mina's seemingly perfect life and husband Jonathan, too. As these troubled characters move ever closer toward their destinies and a final battle with Dracula, blood will be spilled, souls will be destroyed, and love will become undying. Next to zombie films, the erotic lesbian vampire film is the most prolific and maligned genre of low budget filmmaking. Take a few willing actress, some dollar store fangs, stage blood, and bam! you've got a movie, not always a good movie, but a movie. Many of these basement productions are missing essential good film ingredients such as scripts, direction, and talented casts. As many of these films are strictly softcore eye candy and stroke material that can be forgiven. Unfortunately the recent glut of product has resulted in many stale and unsexy efforts with lackluster performances from bored women and camera work that focuses more on elbows and knees than tits and twats.

One of the biggest and best purveyors of the genre is Seduction Cinema, who produced winners such as *An Erotic Vampire in Paris*, and *Vampire's Seduction* (both with the lovely Tina Krause) and *Erotic Rites of Countess Dracula* as well as losers like *Titanic 2000*.

Seduction Cinema's latest addition to the genre is *Lust for Dracula* from director Tony Marsiglia. This may be their most erotic title to date and I believe the first genuinely erotic lesbian vampire masterpiece of this or the last decade. It's an off kilter fever dream fueled by images of sex, beauty and bloodshed much like the seventies lesbian vampire classics of Jean Rollin and the blood splattered *Vampyres: Daughters of Darkness*.

I believe the key to the film's success is due in part to the film's super-sexy, uninhibited cast headlined by Misty Mundae, Darian Caine, Julian Wells, and Shelly Jones. These Seduction staple players are supported by some very lusty performances by Andrea Davis and Casey Jones, whose hot raw girl-on-girl scenes nearly steal the show. Misty gives it her all, as always, playing Mina and Darian Caine makes an interesting Dracula, but top honors go to Julian Wells for her gender-bending take on Jonathan Harker.

The rest of the credit for this fine film goes to Tony Marsiglia who really crafted a fine love letter to classic era lesbian vampire films complete with mounds of naked flesh and a complex dream like abstract plotting. Review based on the unrated DVD version. All in all top notch soft-core action. (MH)

**The Mummy's Kiss (2003)** D. Donald F. Glut. 3000 years ago, an evil Egyptian sorceress, Hor-Shep-Sut, was buried alive for indulging forbidden pleasures of the flesh… with the Pharaoh's beautiful daughter! Now Hor-Shep-Sut's recently excavated Mummy has arrived in modern-day Los Angeles, and the removal of a gold Osiris death mask brings her back to life in all her sensual lesbian splendor.

With the help of a zombified servant, Hor-Shep-Sut must find and reclaim the reincarnation of her ancient lost love whose spirit resides in a luscious archaeology student named Ana. Along the way, she seduces several female students who will-ingly offer their taut young bodies completely to the scheming, pleasure-seeking sorceress. Ana, too begins to ache for the lustful and erotic touch of Hor-Shep-Sut, not knowing who she really is and that they once had been eager lovers in another life. As Ana moves closer towards her fateful yet luxurious encounter with Hor-Shep-Sut, will Ana's fiancée or her uncle, Prof. Wallis Harwa (Richard Lynch) be able to save her?

I think I may have viewed just about every soft-core lesbian vampire film made in the last few years so it was a refreshing change to view *Kiss of the Mummy*. For one it's only the second lesbian mummy film I've seen (there seems to be three so far but I have yet to see the third). Secondly, *Mummy's Kiss* was directed by Don Glut, whose last film, *Erotic Rites of Countess Dracula* (a lesbian vampire film, go figure) I had quite enjoyed. In fact I was actually looking forward the proposed sequel to *Erotic Rites of Countess Dracula*, which was put on hold in order to make this.

*Mummy's Kiss* is a loving tribute to the universal mummy films of old spiced up with tons of nudity and soft-core lesbian. It includes many nods to these classic films and others, including opening with Swan Lake (which was played in the original Boris Karloff *Mummy* film) and the spike mask sequence from Black Sunday. There are also in-jokes to many of Don Glut's other films including *Dinosaur Valley Girls, Erotic Rites of Countess Dracula* and an old mummy film Don made years ago.

The cast is decent is decent and very nice to look at. The film was well shot, edited, has keen special effects (for it's budget) and has some cool locations.

*Mummy's Kiss* is a solid B-film with wall-to-wall nudity as Sasha Peralta, Ava Niche and Aysia Lee make for great window dressing (and they are good actress to boot), action, and a swell story. (MH)

***Pervirella*** ***(1997)*** Written, Directed and Produced by Alex Chandon and Josh Collins. Star-ring Emily Bouffante, Eileen Daily, David Warbeck, Sexton Ming, Jonathan Ross, Mark Lamarr. Did you ever sit down to watch a movie and say to yourself about five minutes in "I'm really not in the mood for this?" That was the feeling I got while watching *Pervirella*.

Around the half-hour mark I realized that I couldn't imagine a time when I *would* be in the mood to watch this movie. Incoherent and shoddily made, shot on 16mm under what must have been the absolute worst of circumstances, *Pervirella* is trying very hard to be about …something. Obviously a parody of the Roger Vadim/Jane Fonda movie *Barbarella* (and not the source comic book that is infinitely more entertaining), *Pervirella* takes place sometime in the future, where an eternal and rotting Queen Victoria rules the land and sex has been outlawed. A young woman with an insatiable sexual appetite is born and, after maturing at an alarming rate from infant to voluptuous adulthood, she joins her surrogate scientist father and a team of misfits on an ill-defined adventure to jungles and far-off lands that look

like they were all set in one room.

The acting and sexual shenanigans in *Pervirella* are over-the-top without being entertaining or even remotely amusing. The only laugh it got out of me was towards the beginning, when very obvious models were used for cityscapes and flying industrial cars. I appreciated the cheesiness of the settings. The rest was just shrill and annoying.

Actors Warbeck and Ross are wasted, Bouffante's frequent nudity actually becomes boring, and every scene makes you wonder if you'd somehow missed something, as not a single thing makes any bit of sense. It's not fun, it's not shocking; it's just irritating. Don't come crying to me if you decide to watch it and something inside of you dies. (MW)

***TITanic 2000 (aka Titanic Vampire).*** D. John P. Fedele. Originally released under the title *Titanic Vampire 2000*, *TITanic 2000* is a new entry in the weird sub-genre that seems to have cropped up over the last four years, namely the Lesbian Vampire Film. Most of these "entertainments" involve naked women with bad vampire fangs, writhing around on the floor with other non-clad women. Usually these films are accompanied by one or two minutes of "plot" to justify the masturbation material.

This latest release from E.I. was probably born like this: Fedele and Zack Snygg were sitting around watching *The Vampire's Seduction* and one turned to the other and said, "What if we did an erotic vampire movie with a story?" Then they most likely got drunk and hammered out this little gem. *Titanic 2000* uses the similar trappings of naked women, the fake fangs better than average, but throws in an ambitious plot and a cast

of amusing –and in a few cases, downright hysterical –characters that creates a whole new beast out of the tired and familiar.

Like *The Vampire's Seduction, Titanic* 2000 involves a female lesbian vampire with tan lines, Vladamina, played by Tammy Parks (The Slice Girls[9]). She and her bizarre henchmen board the newly christened TITanic (yes, that's how it's pronounced, too), along with several other wackos, headed for predictable disaster. Set in the titular year (no pun intended thistime), the newly christened luxury cruiser of the title sets sail, its passengers include an artist (Zachary Winston Snygg), a boozing rock star (the always hilarious John P. Fedele), his girlfriend Wendy (b-movie starlet Tina Krause) and, of course, the vampiric nymph, Countess Vladimina, (the usually nude Tammy Parks).

The surprise comes not from the plot (lesbian couplings, women in various states of undress, the ship sinks), but from the fact that the film is funny. Really funny. There isn't a single scene that takes itself seriously. In fact, the filmmakers, including producer Mike Raso and director Fedele, overload the numerous sequences with sight gags and one-liners that embrace the movie's low budget. For example, as the artist convinces Tina Krause to pose for him, his transition line to cover a continuity error: "Great, let me change into a blue shirt and we'll head over to my cabin." (My second favorite example comes from scream queen Parks to Krause: "The ship's sinking! We have to take off our dresses and swim for it!") Now with sets consisting of blocky computer-generated shots of the ship and various motel rooms, the TITanic rolls full-speed ahead, spoofing everything in sight. The sight-gags come fast, and if you don't laugh at one, you get hit with three more ten seconds later. The actors all seem to be having a blast, especially when the moment arrives for the famed ship to sink (I'm not giving too much away here, am I?). The whole movie looks like it cost about fifteen dollars, and the erotic content is actually secondary here, almost an afterthought, but you'll be too busy laughing to notice. Movies with heart and a sense of humor tend to overcome their budgetary restrictions. Give this one a chance when you're not feeling pretentious. (MW)

***Vampire Obsession (2002)*** D. John Bacchus. Wendy (Anoushka) is a sinfully gorgeous prostitute who lives with her girlfriend (Darian Caine)—an obsessed beauty who desires Wendy all to herself. But when Wendy is propositioned by a mysterious woman named Alexis (Jade DuBoir), things will change forever.

---

[9] "The Slice Girls" were a one-off parody of "The Spice Girls", created by John Russo (*Night of the Living Dead*) and Vlad Licina (*Night of the Living Dead: 30th Anniversary*). The singers included Debbie Rochon ("Isis Slice"), Steffanie Pitt ("Vampee Slice"), Tammy Parks ("Kraftee Slice"), and Christine Cavalier ("Franken Slice").

Seduced in ways she never thought possible, Wendy soon finds herself the love-slave of Alexis who has a taste for bringing home a new woman for them to share every night. Alexis has another bizarre taste too, and she introduces Wendy to her sensual and orgiastic blood fetish. At first resistant, Wendy is quickly turned on by the intoxicating mixture of erotic lesbian pleasures, and finds her own indulgence turning to something much more sinister. Tracked down and confronted by her frantic, sex-starved girlfriend, Wendy must decide if her dark, lustful, body-quivering obsession has gone beyond the edge of sanity—or if her craving for non-stop pleasure has yet to be satisfied. I cannot tell you how thrilled I was when I watched this and it wasn't the same lesbian vampire movie we always get. Finally we're getting some decent plot with our soft-core. The girls all seem to be into their performances, both sexual and acting. Major props to Darian Caine, who turns in probably the flick's best performance as a girl with some *serious* abandonment issues. I'm looking forward to future releases of this level of quality and not more crap with bored-looking chicks with glued-in fangs. Funny thing I was

wondering: How low on the hooker totem pole must Wendy be to be stuck with the graveyard as her territory? (MG)

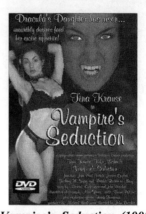

**The Vampire's Seduction (1998)** D. Michael Beckerman. In this early shot-on-video E.I. production, Tina Krause stars as "Dracoola", the last descendent of Dracula, who hypnotizes Wally Van Helsing (John P. Fedele) to do her bidding, namely: "Bring me my lesssbians!" We follow Wally around, as he sneaks into one house after another and spies on half-naked women making out with each other. A little while later, Frankenstein shows up to bop him on the head. Then Frankenstein leaves. Then Wally and Tina do a little dance. Then there's more nudity. Then it's over. (I won't give away the shocking twist ending!) For a movie with absolutely nothing going on save writhing, *The Vampire's Seduction* has a lot going for it. For one thing, it's hilarious. Particularly the opening scene in a diner, where Wally and his social worker (Zack Snygg) annoy a waitress played by Debbie Rochon. Fedele on his own is almost painfully funny, and Tina Krause deserves some points for attempting a Bela Lugosi accent while running round topless in the New Jersey woods (with tan lines, no less. Where does a vampire get tan lines?) This is a great starting point for a drunken movie bash. (MW)

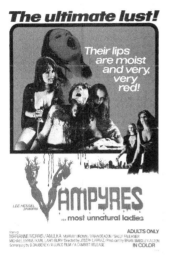

**Vampyres** (1974). D. José Ramón Larraz. Two mysterious women, Fran (Marianne Morris) and Miriam (Anulka Dziubinska, credited as Anulka), live in a mouldering tomb of a lodge home. At night, they pose as hitch-hikers to lure unsuspecting Good Samaritans back to their beds to be devoured. They later stage car-wrecks to explain the mutilated state of their victims' bodies. Fran takes an inexplicable shine to one such would-be victim, Ted (Murray Brown), and she keeps him in a weakened, anemic state shut up in a bedroom. Miriam is appalled. During a shower sequence, she tells Fran they're "playing a dangerous game" and begs her to kill Ted. Meanwhile, the bodies are starting to pile up.

Another film to begin with the journey of a young, happy couple, in this case John and Harriett (Brian Deacon and Sally Faulkner), *Vampyres* quickly dispenses of the straight white couple and spends the majority of its time with its vampyre

lovers. As is also usual with this type of film, neither of the sensuous ladies can convince the audience of their mutual attraction. The lesbian couplings are heavy on caressing, light on the kissing—lots of tongue-touching, a sure sign of the leads' heterosexuality. But where the film fails in the eroticism, it excels is in the horror department. When the bloodlust takes over, the ladies become savage. Even minus fangs, they tear into their victims, gouging trenches into flesh and licking blood off the faces of their prey. There are at least four sequences where the vampyres turn feral as if a switch had been flipped, making each murder frightening to behold.

Filmed on a shoestring inside the Oakley Court lodge and grounds, made famous during the Hammer years and infamous in *The Rocky Horror Picture Show*, director Larraz keeps the camera moving gracefully over the rotting dark wood interiors and misty forests outside. In several shots, the actors don't behave and wander in and out of frame, but Harry Waxman, whose photography on *The Wicker Man* gave that film much of its respectability, does his best to keep up with the action, while giving the bedroom scenes a matter-of-fact moodiness that off-sets the softer "fantasy" of the woods.

Produced by Brian Smedley-Aston (best-known as an editor,

*Anulka Dziubinska and Marianne Morris in Vampyres. Copyright Cambist Films / Cinépix Film Properties Inc.*

whose work on the Donald Cammell/Nicholas Roeg/Mick Jagger phantasmagoria, *Performance* helped craft thatfilm into the psychedelic gangster epic it is today), who kept the cash flowing to ensure Larraz's vsion, *Vampyres* has become infamous over the years, less for its actual eroticism but for the perceived amount of "excised" material unable to be seen legitimately for many years, thanks to UK censors demanding more than five minutes' worth of cuts to the film. This "lost" footage was discussed in hushed tones for years, in magazines and, later, fistfight-inducing message boards. When Blue Underground brought the uncut version to DVD in 2010, it put to rest the pontification that hardcore scenes had been filmed to pad out the running time. While some of the nudity is explicit—the implied oral gratification during the shower scene, the brief appearance of a penis during another sex scene—it still remains in the soft core neighborhood. The savagery of the murders remained unsettling.

By their own accounts, neither Morris nor Anulka were experienced actresses at the time. While Anulka (then famous as the May 1973 *Playboy* Playmate of the Month) went on to become a celebrated commercial model and made appearances in *Lizstomania* and *The New Avengers,* she retired to the life of a "floral designer". Morris made a couple of brief film appearances before herself retiring to raise a family. What neither knew—until Severin honcho David Gregory showed up to interview them for the Blue Underground DVD—was that their voices had been post-dubbed (by Georgia Brown and Annie Ross) on demand by Larraz. Well-made and largely coherent, *Vampyres* for many

set the template for lesbian vampire films—the lonely sirens desperate for food but loving only each other, preying on passers-by. How "good" or "bad" these movies are, seems to be irrelevant. (MW)

***Vampyros Lesbos (1971).*** D. Jess Franco. *Vampyros Lesbos* is a thinly veiled rehash of *Dracula* that starts with a beautiful American lawyer Linda Westinghouse having constant sensuous dreams of erotic lesbian couplings with a dark haired lover she has never met. She shares this dream with her therapist, who suggests she needs a better lover in a way that sounds like a come on. Shortly after that, Linda is assigned to resolve an inheritance issue with the Countess Nadine Carody. Wishing to deal with the Countess directly Linda travels to Nadine's island home (apparently Dracula's beach bungalow) where it turns out the Countess is her mysterious dream lover...

It's a dreamy tale of vampire lust set on the very sunny coast of Turkey, making it the most sundrenched tale of vampirism I have seen, save for the desert-set *The Velvet Vampire*. Being on the sunny seashore, it trades beach houses and pools for graveyards and castles, high flying kites for bats and fishing nets for cobwebs.

The film stars Soledad Miranda (Jess Franco's muse at the time), a very European ice queen beauty, and statuesque blond Ewa Strömberg. Dennis Price, Paul Muller, and Andrea Montchal also are on hand in some thankless roles that go almost nowhere.

One of the biggest complaints levied against Jess Franco's *Vampyros Lesbos* by critics and casual fans alike is that the film is boring (a crime of many of his films to be sure). Indeed the film can be quite laborious especially in a world of laptops, smart phones, and tablets; but oddly enough in this case it seems that boring is what Jess was shooting for. He was not trying to tell a tale of red hot vampire blood lust or even a simple bit of lesbian softcore titillation. Win or lose he had grander plans for the film and offered up a study of the soul crushing ennui brought on by vampirism's eternal damnation and everlasting immortality.

He does not accomplish this so much in the traditional way of script and story—though the dubbing offers up some odd echoes that make it seem more dreamlike in places—instead he offers up a treasure trove of puzzling visual set pieces, flying kites, hostel scorpions, cold, almost-necromantic lovemaking and some very strange dance/stripper routines at a nightclub featuring the stunning Soledad Miranda and Heidrun Kussin as Agra, her mannequin/Renfield. It's the kind of visual smorgasbord that could feed a whole film class full of thesis.

But hey, there is more to *Vampyros Lesbos* than just its appearance the film also boasts a great psychedelic sound-track, with all tracks written by written by Manfred Hübler and Siegfried Schwab. In fact it was super popular in Great Britain and can be still obtained easily on CD to this day, look for it by name, "*Vampyros Lesbos: Sexadelic Dance Party,*" and score your own copy! The CD also features music from *Vampyros Lesbos'* sister film *She Killed in Ecstasy* and *The Devil Came from Akasava*. (MH)

*Soledad Miranda stars in the Jess Franco fever dream, **Vampyros Lesbos**.*
*Photo Copyright Fénix Films. All Rights reserved*

# I'd Buy That For a Dollar!

Mike Haushalter

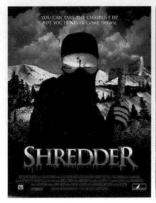  

One of my favorite activities is to look through bargain bins and the racks of second-hand sellers to find movie deals. Whether it's a forgotten A-list title, blink and you missed it indie release, or last year's hot direct to home video title, as long as it costs 2 to 5 bucks it's bound to come home with me. But if it's less than that? Well, I'm willing to take a gamble on almost anything that's priced at a dollar and offers even a tiny bit of intrigue or interest. After all, I can't even rent most of these things for that price, and if they don't work out, I can sell them again. But when they do work out, it's magical. Here's a roundup of my latest finds, good and bad (mostly bad this time out).

### Shredder (2003)

**The box says:** Horror hits the slopes in this sexy slasher film about a gang of snowboarders on a one way chair lift to horror! Featuring hot young stars, killer suspense, and snowboarding sequences to die for, *Shredder* is an ice-cold rip-roaring scare-fest that takes terror to a whole new altitude.

**Why I risked a dollar:** A slasher film killing off snowboarders? That's no brainer must see tv!

Besides, who could pass this up after reading that ad copy above?

**Thoughts:** The first 5 minutes or so we're kind of rocky and I thought I had picked a total bomb but things quickly smoothed out as I realized the filmmakers knew they were stuck with a dud idea (and not too much snow at their location). They did their best to at least make it a fun time waster if not a worthwhile one.

**Plus:** A few decent gore effects, sense of humor and a bit of T&A for for the lads and some guy booty for the ladies

**Minus:** Less than satisfactory villain reveal, nauseating editing in some of the snowboarding scenes, Troma rejected Thrash Core music cues, and the subject matter is a bit beyond its expiration date.

**Shelf/Bin:** Bin: I was really starting to warm up to the thought that this might be a keeper and then it just kind of crapped out in the last 10 or so minutes so it's going in the bin.

### Dark Blue (2003)

**The box says:** From the writer of *Training Day* comes "this terrific corrupt-cop drama" (Entertainment Weekly) set in the days leading up to the LA riots.Starring Kurt Russell

82

(*Escape From New York*) and a acclaimed ensemble this gritty police thriller "keeps you on the edge of your seat with white knuckle suspense" (The New York Observer).

Adrenaline is high, tempers are hot and racial tensions are boiling over.Against this explosive backdrop, LAPD detective Eldon Perry (Russell) tutors his rookie partner (Scott Speedman) in the realities of police intimidation and corruption as they investigate a high profile homicide case. But as the body count rises- and the evidence just doesn't add up- Assistant chief Arthur Holland (Ving Rhames) threatens to end Perry's brand of "justice"... If Perry's own demons don't end him first.

**Why I risked a dollar:** Well the larger than life looking Kurt Russell on the front was hard to pass up. When I read the synopsis and cast list I realized that this film had the potential of perhaps being a forgotten good film that slipped through the cracks.

**Thoughts**: his was an honest to goodness good movie well worth a dollar and probably worthy of a much more in depth and thought out review but judging from the amount of quotes on the box I am sure my review can wait. The film is set in Los Angeles during the trial of the police officers that assaulted Rodney King. It is shot in a way that makes it feel raw and uncomfortable, that makes you somewhat disturbed by how real what you are seeing could be. It boggles my mind that in 2003 people still would

have wanted a pan and scan version of a film to watch.

**Plus:** Great cast. Great script.

**Minus:** Many years later and this film just hits too close to home to be completely enjoyable for my tastes.

**Shelf/Bin:** Unsure: The dvd has audio commentary so we will give it at least one more view.

### Old 37 (2015)

**What the box says:** Deep down the forgotten stretches of back road where the cool kids race their cars, two deranged brothers, Darryl (Bill Moseley, *The Devil's Reject*s) and Jon Roy (Kane Hodder, *Hatchet*) intercept 911 calls in their father's beat up old ambulance to exact medical atrocities upon their unlucky victims

**Why I risked a dollar:** Thought it looked like a possible shot at a convention made train wreck starring Bill Moseley and Kane Hodder

**Thoughts:** It's a very bad sign when the credits begin with an Alan Smithee film. It's a bitter movie about shallow people that for the most part deserve to die. I also wonder if they paid Kane Hodder too little to speak or if they paid him extra not to speak.

**Plus:** Some very brutal gore. Decent work from Bill Moseley.

**Minus**: Some of the least likeable characters ever to be on screen.Just really had rough time giving a damn about any of these assclowns.

**Shelf/bin**: Bin: Straight to bin, do not pass go, do not collect $200 dollars.

# LEGWORK

By Bill Homan

So they needed some broad for a shoot. "Just make sure she has great legs!" they said. I figure it's no problem, I'm the casting guy after all. I see dames come in here all the time with great legs. Sometimes that's all you even see on 'em, or want to anyway. So I put out the call, any ladies may apply. You have to be politically correct these days, you know. I figured I'd just scope 'em as they came and see what kind of gams I could pull out of the no talent riff-raff that come in here trying to sell themselves every freakin' day.

Somehow they must have known. Somehow they knew I'd just be lookin' at their legs, to hell with talent and other good looks. So that's all that showed up, legs! Oh sure, there were hips attached, this one broad even had enough belly that I could see her naval ring. But right after that, every one of 'em, sheared right off. Some of 'em were nice and cleanly cut, others were just a torn, jagged mess with blood and intestines looped over the waist like some off-the-rack belt. Now, I'm not a prejudiced guy, but even I get a little uneasy when half a woman walks in and first thing you see is her spleen.

I tried to take it in stride (no pun intended), but the whole day just turned into one big mess. First off, none of these gals had arms or hands for the paperwork. I couldn't even get any names out of 'em! I'd ask about experience and they would just stand there and- nothing... Like it was my fault they didn't have mouths or lungs to talk with. They were tripping over themselves to get my attention though. I finally resorted to a number system and those yellow stick notes. Some of the broads thought I was trying to get fresh with where I stuck their little yellow tag. Now you know me, the soul of professionalism here. Like anyone else in town is even auditioning the lower halves of women!

Well, I'd had as much as I was willing to take for one day, so I politely told them all I'd be in touch. I'm not really sure how they heard me, but at least they couldn't slam the door. I decided on two or three of these gals for tomorrow's casting meeting. I was finally heading home after two hours of overtime, that group took a lot of work. But it's OK, the missus will understand.

She's all heart.

# PARTING SHOT
## By Mike Watt

I know, who does an "afterward" for a magazine? What? Did you just have pages to fill? Yes. Yes, I did. That being said, with the final looks taken at the publication you currently hold in your hands, I was struck with the desire to examine the "why" of it all? What is the hold that "exploitation films" still have over the film fan?

Let's be honest with ourselves. Most exploitation films—or "grindhouse films" or "B-grade" to "Z-Grade"—are not very good. Many don't even fall into the category of "so bad they're good." From the spate of drive-in bound horror, women-in-prison, "hick-sploitation", "nun-sploitation", etc., given to us in the '70s, through the shot-on-video slasher craze of the late-'80s, we all have our favorites, but taken objectively, the bulk of these titles are underlit, poorly filmed, wretchedly acted, rife with spurious "special" effects. Hell, we consider ourselves lucky if the boom mike doesn't become its own character. Take into account that these films celebrate the worst of human behavior for the sake of "entertainment," and the questions become more numerous. Why do we return time and again to this well? Why do we continue to plumb the depths of the low brow?

It's a question I frequently ask myself twice a year as I help put together Pete Chiarella's *Grindhouse Purgatory*, itself an even-more exuberant celebration of the sleazy knock-offs that permeated theaters, particularly during New York's wonderfully shameless hey-day of 42$^{nd}$ Street. Why do we celebrate what most "normal" people would dismiss as crap? Are we all hearty mavericks, eager to explore the deepest crevices of filmmaking? Does this give us special insight into film history that may otherwise elude the more casual film fan? Maybe it does and maybe it doesn't. We certainly act that way online. Nobody is quicker to fight another's opinion faster than a film fan.

Part of the appeal of the grindhouse movie is the subversive nature inherent in the movie. These films are rarely parades thrown in honor of the virtuous. The dominant theme running throughout these independently-shot features is the "corruption, seduction, or destruction of the innocent." They are generally reflections of our own base nature, and our enjoyment stems from our ability to separate ourselves from the worst of the antagonists, while still allowing our ids to feed on the (sometimes laughable but more often horrifying) suffering of the victims. Why do we need this outlet?

It's not even a new question. Paw through the history of any popular entertainment and you'll see the violent, questionable roots of the morality tale overcome by its prurient elements. The Brothers Grimm were excoriated for celebrating the violence of peasants following the publication of their first collection of folk tales. Yet, Jacob and Wilhelm took great pains to "soften" the more horrific elements in deference to their target audience of children. The tale of *Cinderella* as per the Grimms, with the evil Stepmother bound in red-hot iron shoes and birds sent to peck out the eyes of the stepsisters (after they mutilate their feet to fit into the fabulous abandoned slipper, blood pouring over the sides of the shoe)—

think what it must have been *prior* to their more gentle telling. In fact, look no further than *Der Struwwelpeter* (aka *Shockheaded Peter*) is a German children's book by Heinrich Hoffmann. Published in 1845, 33 years after the Grimms' first edition, originally titled *Lustige Geschichten und drollige Bilder mit 15 schön kolorierten Tafeln für Kinder von 3–6 Jahren* (*Funny Stories and Whimsical Pictures with 15 Beautifully Coloured Panels for Children Aged 3 to 6*), included are such tales as a roving tailor who slices off the offending digits of thumb-sucking children, or kids who are taught the evils of racism by being dipped in black ink. The Germans are such a comforting people.

We talk of "shock value", of "selling the sizzle, not the steak," to justify when the elements of misery are stronger than the story. That's the heart of the exploitation film: the violence, the gore, the nudity, the violence again. That's the sizzle. The steak is secondary. What the hell is *Raw Force* about beyond a barely-functioning drunken Cameron Mitchell battling ninjas in the Philippines? Nobody knows, nor cares. That's not the sizzle.

The appetite for the vile and pernicious in entertainment might predate written history. Hell, read the Bible and fulfill your need for antisocial behavior, sometimes punished, sometimes merely implied, but details rarely spared. It's the allure of the forbidden. Parents groups make for great outcry for censorship, which governments are always too eager to answer. Every day, we're told we can't do this or that, though not by censorship laws (at least in this country), but by our fellow citizens. Think of this group's feelings, their history of oppression. Think of the ramifications on society if "x" is celebrated even in passing. Every element of our culture is at war with one subgroup or another. And while most of us try to be good people in "real" life, it's exhausting, it's aggravating. In response, we rail against the invasion of "Politically Correct (P.C.) Culture". Watch what you say, watch what you do, be careful of what you love.

The exploitation film imposes no such restriction on us. The majority of film fans understand that the title character of *Ilsa: She Wolf of the SS* is not the hero of the film. Her barbaric practices are not to be duplicated. We said "never again" after the closing of the death camps in Germany. But we still have a fascination with the grotesque; it's the darkness present in every person's soul, whether they choose to acknowledge it or not. Only a miniscule minority of film lovers would try to emulate the acts we witness on film. In fact, we make more movies about that minority of misanthropic creeps; look no further than that pair of atrocities, *Human Centipede II: the Centipeding*, or *A Serbian Film,* to plumb the depths of our psyche and see it reflected back.

But the films themselves are rarely morality tales beyond the inevitable deaths of the protagonists or anti-heroes. *Vanishing Point*'s Kowalski (Barry Newman) final act of defiance that leads to his demise comes as much from his personal need for self-destruction than it is a demand of the society he's rebelling against. Even Krug and Company in the aforementioned *Last House on the Left* are rebelling against "the Man". And sometimes the anti-social behavior speaks to us. We don't have to be "P.C." during a screening of *I*

*Spit on Your Grave* to root for Camille Keaton's eventual revenge. She went through hell and back and those that dragged her along that trip deserve everything they get. And when they do, our primal forms celebrate. Our Jungian shadowforms dance once more around the bonfire. The exploitation film never asks us to examine our responses. The exploitation film doesn't ask anything more than our attention. There is rarely a message. "Young girl gets mixed up in the wrong crowd and is either corrupted or destroyed. Regardless, in the end, she will not be the same." That's the sum total of the messages most exploitation films will even attempt to deliver. "Crime doesn't pay," barely even registers because the crime is usually the impetus to the retribution. Better might be the message: "No one here gets out alive. Good, bad, or indifferent, we're all wearing a pine box at the end." Honestly, there's something comforting in that.

You can debate all day long the "value" of such films—as films, as messages sent or received, as excoriation of women, as celebration of the criminal—but in the end, all the movies ask are "are you not entertained?" Exploitation movies rarely carry baggage. They are what they are and don't even pretend to be anything else. Are women-in-prison movies spotlights on the corruption of our prison system? Maybe via lip-service. Mostly, they're excuses for cat fights, whipping, lesbianism, nudity, and final apocalyptic revenge. As theatrical director Moss Hart once said, "If you want to send a message, try Western Union. I'm telling a story."

Exploitation Films are little more than a rush of adrenaline and an appeal to the repressed id. The values of the outside world are set aside for roughly 80 minutes of fist fights, shootouts, decapitations, rape, murder, and vengeance. They fall into the purest forms of fantasy: one that asks very little of the viewer in return.

In the exploitation realms, there is no shame. Exploitation means only that. Never calls for higher consciousness. Indeed, their *raison d'etre* is to warn us that violence is inevitable, but if our only encounter is in the cinema, we might get a little farther than the people who want to pretend it doesn't exist at all, or that their own psyches are somehow "above it all".

Yes, we love our blockbuster superhero movies, but sometimes we need that dose of the ultraviolence to get our blood moving again. And because there are no rules to an exploitation film beyond the exploitation, you never really know where the film is going to go. That's why the ending of *The Candy Snatchers* is so gutting. It didn't play fair or ascribe to the rules handed down by the censors or the Hays Code. Indeed, after decades of self-censorship, exploitation grew out of the need for less sanitized fare, and that need is still strong in all of us today.

In the outside world, we have to be kind and understanding. We hold doors for people; we don't aim our cars at pedestrians in the parking lot. We hold our own views on what is virtuous and good for society. We take part in arguments for and against abortion, same-sex marriage, civil rights and equality. And we turn to the exploitation film to see the oppressed minority of one or two overcoming (or not) the odds of societal norms or the perverters of such. We ignore the production values and make heroes out of guys like Jess Franco aand who is anyone else to tell us we're wrong.

It's the contradiction that the best among us find solace in the basest of entertainment. It's not something we feel the need to apologize for and few of us even take the time to examine our attraction to the horror and misanthropy. We are not blind to the genuine horrors that exist in real life, and combat it when and where we can. But with exploitation cinema, we are here to be entertained, not educated. And for a very few of us, there is the hope that the cinematic violence is as close as we'll ever get to the real thing. The exploitation film is the roller coaster ride of morality. We will not choose to be the monster, but for a few minutes in the dark, we can root for the evil and be absolved by the credit scroll. We will defend the indefensible. We will pretend to be savvy and educated and *civilized* once the lights come back up. Until then, we will embrace the mad killer and the lesbian vampire. We will wallow in the excess.

We will relish the escape.

## ABOUT OUR CONTRIBUTORS:

**Bill Adcock** was raised on a steady diet of old monster movies and just look what it did to him. Self-described as reclusive and long-suffering, he requires little provocation to go off at length about gorilla suits, gill-men, and the filmography of Uschi Digard. When not watching utter trash, he can be found talking to his cat like it's people.

**Dr. Rhonda Baughman** is a writer and educator, currently resides in Colorado Springs, CO. She has written for *Sirens of Cinema, Film Threat, Grindhouse Purgatory,* and is the author of the novella, *My Transvestite: A Novella of Love and Death, Pornography and Revolution.*

**David Cooper** is an acclaimed Pittsburgh-based photographer. More of his work can be found at www.davidcooperphoto.com.

**Matt Gilligan** lives in Pittsburgh, Pennsylvania and works as a graphic designer and web developer. He has previously written for *Secret Scroll Digest* and was zombie in a Mike Watt film..

**Mike Haushalter** is a lifetime fan and student of film. A genre film reviewer for *Drive-In Asylum, Grindhouse Purgatory*, and *Weng's Chop*. He is the publisher, writer, and publicity for *Secret Scroll Digest.*

**Bill Homan** is a special effects artist, puppeteer, cryptozoologist, and one of the founders of Happy Cloud Pictures.

**Ryan Hose** is a graphic designer and illustrator in the Pittsburgh area, specializing in vector graphics, pencil renderings, and quirky layouts. He will talk endlessly about music. Check out his portfolio at behance.net/ryandennis923f

**Douglas Waltz** resides in the wilds of Kalamazoo Michigan and when he's not working on his own 'zine, *Divine Exploitation,* he contributes to *Grindhouse Purgatory, Monster!, Weng's Chop.* In the land of fiction his recent releases are *Thou Shalt Not Live!, Sasquatch Vs. The Blind Dead* and *Killer F\*\*king Squirrels.*

**William J. Wright** is a Rondo Hatton Classic Horror Award nominated journalist and critic specializing in horror and cult entertainment. His work has appeared in *Phantom of the Movies' Videoscope, Penny Blood, Sirens of Cinema, Fangoria.com, Stiff, Dread Central* and *Film Threat,* among others. In addition to his print work, he produces and co-hosts the MORTIS horror podcast. (wm.j.wright@gmail.com, mortiscontact@gmail.com)

**NEXT ISSUE: Bigfoot, The Mothman, and Cryptozology in Cinema**

22296708R00051

Printed in Poland
by Amazon Fulfillment
Poland Sp. z o.o., Wrocław